Be Angry and Sin Not

*– Do Not Let the Sun Go
Down on Your Wrath!*
Ephesians 4:26

Warren Henderson

All Scripture quotations from the King James Version of the Bible unless otherwise noted.

Be Angry and Sin Not
By Warren Henderson
Copyright © 2005

Published by Gospel Folio Press
304 Killaly Street West
Port Colborne, ON, L3K 6A6, Canada

ISBN 1-882701-

ORDERING INFORMATION:
Gospel Folio Press
Phone 1-905-835-9166
E-mail: order@gospelfolio.com

Printed in the United States of America

Contents

Acknowledgements

The author is profoundly grateful to all those who sacrificed their time and talents to aid the publishing of *Be Angry and Sin Not*. I thank the Lord for each of the following and their contributions: Dāveen Lidstone for cover design and layout. David Dunlap, and Mike Attwood for technical editing. Jane Biberstein for general editing. Annette Hanson, David Lindstrom, Gina Mulligan, and my dear wife Brenda for proofreading assistance.

Preface

"For the wrath of man worketh not the righteousness of God" (Jas. 1:20). Aristotle delineated man's inherent propensity to mishandle anger: "Anybody can become angry. That is easy. But to be angry with the right person and to the right degree and at the right time and for the right purpose and in the right way – that is not within everybody's power and is not easy."[1] Anger is one of the most powerful and assertive emotions God conferred to mankind on the day He breathed into Adam's nostrils the breath of life. Anger would enable man to serve God and his fellowman during alarming circumstances when other emotions would simply be inadequate.

Anger is an emotion not a behavior. It is neither good nor bad, though it excites good or bad behavior depending upon the spiritual condition of our inner man. For many, anger has become an expensive luxury for selfish abuse. In recent years, the number of individuals in anger counseling has escalated – a ramification of a self-seeking culture. A society characterized by child abuse, immorality, broken homes, disrespect to authority and poor child training is destined to experience an anger epidemic. Recently, the Associated Press reported on a case of restaurant rage where a 34-year-old Houston man, apparently angry that his $6 steak and cheese sandwich was too cold, was arrested on a charge of threatening to blow up the restaurant and kill its manager.[2] From road rage to terrorism, acts of rage

1

dominate our news reports. Anger and death will rule a society that has drifted apart from God, for life and peace are only obtained through Jesus Christ (Jn. 1:4, 16:33).

Without Scripture, mankind would be deficient in properly comprehending what anger is and how it is to be used. Without the indwelling Holy Spirit, the Christian would have no hope of yielding his or her anger to affect righteousness for God's glory. *"Be ye angry, and sin not: let not the sun go down upon your wrath"* (Eph. 4:26)! Commenting on the first portion of this verse, Charles Spurgeon wrote, "There can hardly be goodness in a man if he be not angry at sin; he who loves truth must hate every false way."[3] Righteous anger purposes good and bestows blessing, while unrighteous anger vents wrath and harbors resentment. For the sun to go down upon a settled and peaceful heart, the smoldering embers of resentment and fierce flames of rage must be extinguished.

Anger liberation, emotional healing, and spiritual regeneration are only possible through knowing divine truth and yielding to it. *"And ye shall know the truth, and the truth shall make you free.... If the Son therefore shall make you free, ye shall be free indeed"* (Jn. 8:32, 36). There are many humanistic forms of anger self-helps available today, but as Raymond J. Larson puts it, "Psychotherapy will put a band-aid on the gash; but for healing, men's lives must be changed from within."[4] In the following pages, the reader will first learn of God's desire for anger as seen in His own righteous character and revealed precepts, then tools for bringing wrong anger attitudes in line with His purposes will be offered. For our souls to enjoy serenity, we must cleanse our anger, heal emotional scars, abandon selfish bents, and experience forgiveness, both God's and our own.

Understanding Anger

Anger is often thought of as an undesired and hostile behavior, but this notion is flawed on two counts. First, anger is an emotion, not a behavior, though it usually incites behavior. Secondly, circumstances exist that require anger-motivated behavior to accomplish good. Anger should not be thought of as an evil emotion – it is the wrong choices actualized when one is angry that are harmful. If one chooses to uphold the righteousness of God when angry, then God is honored.

God demonstrates this reality in His own character and behavior. The Old Testament contains over 200 direct and approximately another 150 implied references to divine anger. God's anger is associated with the unrighteous conduct of His creatures that possess a free moral will, namely angels and humans. *"God is angry with the wicked every day"* (Ps. 7:11). God is holy in nature and, therefore, cannot sin (Ps. 30:4, 111:9). *"For the righteous Lord loveth righteousness"* (Ps. 11:7). His very essence defines what is righteous – what is apart from God is unholy (Isa. 45:5-7). That Scripture frequently reveals God's anger as a righteous emotion in response to unholy conduct affirms that anger itself is not a sin. Likewise, from time to time, all of us will be confronted with circumstances that prompt our anger. The challenge is to ensure that our anger will honor God and not needlessly hurt others or serve ourselves.

God integrated the potential for anger within our makeup to achieve critical feats when demanded by arduous situations. Common emotions do not adequately prepare us physiologically to respond at such formidable junctures in time, but stronger feelings like fear and anger do. Charles Dickens illustrates this facet of our anger with vivid literary proficiency in his classic book *Oliver Twist*. Noah, an older and sturdier lad, had ruthlessly insulted Oliver's dead mother:

> Crimson with fury, Oliver started up; overthrew the chair and table; seized Noah by the throat; shook him, in the violence of his rage, till his teeth chattered in his head; and, collecting his whole force into one heavy blow, felled him to the ground.

> A minute ago, the boy had looked the quiet, mild, dejected creature that harsh treatment had made him. But his spirit was roused at last; the cruel insult to his dead mother had set his blood on fire. His breast heaved; his attitude was erect; his eye bright and vivid; his whole person changed, as he stood glaring over the cowardly tormentor who now lay crouching at his feet; and defied him with an energy he had never known before.[1]

If I observed someone physically abusing one of my children, extreme emotions would promptly prepare my body to respond to the vicious assault with profound and rare behavior. Glands throughout my body (the hypothalamus, pituitary, thyroid, adrenal, and others) would disperse a variety of hormones into my blood stream. My sympathetic nervous system would instantly be placed on high alert. My blood pressure and blood sugar levels would surge. Critical organs would be brought to peak capacity. My breathing would quicken and deepen. My heart would more vigorously compel oxygen-enriched blood through my circulatory system. Soon, my muscles would begin to tingle and twitch with the stimulation. Almost immediately and involuntarily, I would feel jittery and shriek with apprehension. For some, these sensations are intoxicating and welcomed, but for others, the frenzy of strong feelings are loathed and detestable. Neither of these responses is appropriate when one has been provoked to anger for a legitimate cause.

Paul exhorted the believers at Ephesus, *"Be ye angry, and sin not; let not the sun go down upon your wrath; neither give place to the devil"* (Eph. 4:26-27). Herein lies the problem. Anger enables me to do the spectacular, but because it is such a powerful emotion, I can have difficulty managing it well for very long. Congealed anger will eventually prompt me to sin against God and hurt others. Anger must be immediately extinguished after it has served God, or it will ultimately serve the flesh.

Be Angry and Sin Not tackles such questions as "Why am I angry?" "Should I be angry?" "How do I control my angry feelings?" and "How can my anger benefit others and serve God?". From Scripture, we will learn of God's holy anger, then commence upon the difficult task of aligning our selfish anger and unrighteous behavior with His righteousness. This task will require each of us to honestly evaluate our anger tendencies, to remove internal conditions that frequently induce angry feelings, and to learn techniques to manage our anger in a God-honoring way. If you mismanage anger, this book will guide you into better self-control.

God's Anger – Our Pattern

It may be observed that Scripture does not mention anger before the fall of man or the rebellion of Lucifer. God is unchanging in every aspect of His essence and character (Mal. 3:6). He, therefore, had the capacity to be angry before He created anything, even though there was no one to be angry with. Adam was fashioned in the "likeness" of God (Gen. 1:26) and, thus, had the inherent capacity to experience anger immediately after God breathed life into his inert form. While man was in Eden, anger was dormant, unneeded and unwelcome.

Man had also been created in God's image to visibly represent God's authority over His creation; thus, he was God's crown to creation (Heb. 2:7-8). As long as upright and innocent man maintained a pure testimony of God's authority in creation, a state of felicity existed in Eden for there was nothing present to provoke anger. We may conclude, therefore, that all anger manifests itself righteously or unrighteously as a result of wrongdoing – sin. Sin provokes anger and, if not managed, anger incites more sin – it is a vicious cycle that ensures much suffering and pain.

Before investigating the peculiarities and flaws of our own anger, we need to research God's intent for anger and its proper usage. This objective is best accomplished by examining what God has revealed in Scripture regarding His own anger. The Lord's anger is always perfect and in agreement with His divine character. God is not motivated to action by one particular emotion in such a way that any part of His perfect character is compromised. Love, grace, mercy, justice, righteousness, long-suffering, purity, etc. are always satisfied in every divine action. This is why Paul speaks of the *"fruit of the Spirit"* in Galatians 5:22-23 and not the "fruits of the Spirit." All God's character is homogeneous in reflecting holiness.

Yes, God is a God of love (1 Jn. 4:8), but He could not justly save mankind by love alone – His justice demanded judgment for sin. *"But God commendeth His love toward us, in that, while we were yet sinners, Christ died for us. Much more then, being now justified by His blood, we shall be saved from wrath through Him"* (Rom. 5:8-9). Thus, God's love found a way to righteously offer salvation through judging His Son for human sin. He can legally offer the gift of eternal salvation to *"whosoever will."* Those who reject His gracious offer will spend an eternity in hell, *"for the wages of sin is death"* (Rom. 6:23). "The eternity of punishment is a thought which crushes the heart," said Charles Spurgeon. "The Lord God is slow to anger, but when He is once aroused to it, as He will be against those who finally reject His Son, He will put forth all His omnipotence to crush His enemies."[1]

Perhaps the reader heard the parental instruction during childhood, "do what I say and not what I do." Our heavenly Father can truly charge us to "do what I do and do what I say," for there is no inconsistency between the two. God longs for His children to be like Himself and His Son in thought and deed (Rom. 8:29). *"Be ye holy; for I am holy"* (1 Pet. 1:16).

How is it possible to morally behave as God does? *"But we all, with open face beholding as in a glass the glory of the Lord, are changed into the same image from glory to glory, even as by the Spirit of the Lord"* (2 Cor. 3:18). We can keep our faces

8

unveiled before God by confessing and forsaking sin. Understanding of righteousness is gained from beholding the glass or the mirror (the Word of God – Jas. 1:23-25), so that we can see ourselves in contrast to God's holiness. By yielding to divine truth, the believer is transformed into deeper shades of Christlikeness *(same image from glory to glory)*.

Occupation with the splendor and glory of Christ and submission to the control of the Holy Spirit will truly usher holy living into our lives. H.A. Ironside explains this understanding in his book *Holiness – The False and the True*:

> I have been learning all along my pilgrim journey that the more my heart is taken up with Christ, the more do I enjoy practical deliverance from sin's power, and the more do I realize what it is to have the love of God shed abroad in that heart by the Holy Spirit given to me, as the earnest of the glory to come.[2]

So let us learn the characteristics of God's anger, and pray for grace to conform the working of our anger to His. Living a Christ-centered and disciplined life will reduce the number of occasions on which we inappropriately and unnecessarily feel angry. While in close fellowship with the Lord, the power of the Holy Spirit will effectively control and mold our anger to accomplish the righteousness of God.

God is slow to anger.
The Lord is merciful and gracious, <u>slow to anger</u>, and plenteous in mercy. He will not always chide: neither will He keep His anger forever (Ps. 103:8-9).

The Lord is gracious, and full of compassion; <u>slow to anger</u>, and of great mercy (Ps. 145:8).

Inherently, God is slow to anger, so we should be also. The fact that God's anger is not quickly kindled does not mean He is negligent to act. His slowness to anger ensures a deliberate response at the appropriate time. By His own character, God demonstrates that anger is to be a secondary, not a primary emotion. If anger were a primary emotion, it would rule our lives with a heavy hand. Anger is not to be a quick-triggered emotion that abruptly enters and exits our daily routine. God desires for us to have a long-suffering attitude, which allows anger to deliver a measured response at the most advantageous time.

He that is <u>soon angry</u> dealeth foolishly: and a man of wicked devices is hated (Prov. 14:17).

For a bishop must be blameless, as the steward of God; not selfwilled, <u>not soon angry</u>, not given to wine, no striker, not given to filthy lucre" (Titus 1:7).

He that is <u>slow to anger</u> is better than the mighty; and he that ruleth his spirit than he that taketh a city (Prov. 16:32).

God is provoked to anger.

When thou shalt beget children, and children's children, and ye shall have remained long in the land, and shall corrupt yourselves, and make a graven image, or the likeness of any thing, and shall do evil in the sight of the Lord thy God, <u>to provoke Him to anger</u> (Deut. 4:25)

And I fell down before the Lord, as at the first, forty days and forty nights: I did neither eat bread, nor drink water, because of all your sins which ye sinned, in doing wickedly in the sight of the Lord, <u>to provoke Him to anger</u>. (Deut. 9:18).

The Lord is not a furious God, but He is "provoked" to anger. Either an appalling event or a series of distressing circumstances should occur before anger heightens the body into action. The Lord Jesus said, *"That whosoever is angry with his brother without a cause shall be in danger of the judgment"* (Mt. 5:22). One of the first questions we should ask ourselves when first feeling angry is "Do I have a righteous cause to be angry?" If the situation does not demand anger-induced behavior, we have been wrongly provoked to anger.

Be ye angry, and sin not: let not the sun go down upon your wrath: Neither give place to the devil. (Eph. 4:26-27).

God's anger is kindled.
And the anger of the Lord was kindled against Moses, and He said, Is not Aaron the Levite thy brother? I know that he can speak well. And also, behold, he cometh forth to meet thee: and when he seeth thee, he will be glad in his heart (Ex. 4:14).

And when the people complained, it displeased the Lord: and the Lord heard it; and His anger was kindled; and the fire of the Lord burnt among them, and consumed them that were in the uttermost parts of the camp (Num. 11:1).

The Hebrew word translated as "kindled" in the above verses is *charah* (khaw-raw'), which means "to grow warm." It is normally applied in a figurative sense, "to blaze up." The word describes the igniting of combustible materials and the nursing of the initial spark into the desired conflagration. Not only is God slow to be angry, but once provoked to anger, His anger fully develops before action is rendered. His anger requires sufficient kindling before flaming vengeance is invoked.

11

"Wherefore we receiving a kingdom which cannot be moved, let us have grace, whereby we may serve God acceptably with reverence and godly fear: For our God is a consuming fire" (Heb. 12:28-29). Righteous provocation and a period of anger development is necessary before action is discharged.

God's anger does not endure.

Sing unto the Lord, O ye saints of His, and give thanks at the remembrance of His holiness. For His anger endureth but a moment; in His favour is life: weeping may endure for a night, but joy cometh in the morning (Ps. 30:4-5).

He will not always chide: neither will He keep His anger forever (Ps. 103:9).

Anger must have an immediate God-honoring purpose, or it is to be released. This is a fundamental rule of anger management – my anger must have a **present righteous purpose,** or it must be dismissed until such a time as it can immediately and righteously serve God. Once righteous anger has served God, it also must be relinquished. Anger is too strong of an emotion to contain or control for a long period of time – eventually, we will serve the flesh, and in so doing, we sin against God.

Rest in the Lord, and wait patiently for Him: fret not thyself because of him who prospereth in his way, because of the man who bringeth wicked devices to pass. Cease from anger, and forsake wrath: fret not thyself in any wise to do evil (Ps. 37:7-8).

Be not hasty in thy spirit to be angry: for anger resteth in the bosom of fools (Eccl. 7:9).

God's anger prompts His secondary work.

For the Lord will rise up as at Mount Perazim, He will be angry as in the Valley of Gibeon – that He may do His work, His awesome work, and bring to pass His act, His <u>unusual act</u> (Isa. 28:21 NKJV).

The Lord will rise up as he did at Mount Perazim, He will rouse himself as in the Valley of Gibeon – to do His work, <u>His strange work</u>, and perform His task, <u>His alien task</u> (Isa. 28:21 NIV).

Isaiah calls our attention to the fact that God's anger and subsequent wrath are not part of His primary work. God's anger leading to judgment then destruction is a necessary aspect of God's sovereignty, but His usual and normal work arises from His gracious loving nature. It is not that righteous wrath is less noble than divine love, for each necessitates the other. J. Oswald Sanders explains:

It was Jesus' love for the man with the withered hand that aroused His anger against those who would deny him healing. It was His love for His Father, and zeal for His glory, that kindled His anger against the mercenary traders who had turned His house of prayer for all nations into a cave of robbers (Mt. 21:13, Jn. 2:15-17).[3]

Although Scripture frequently speaks of God's wrath and anger, His actions of mercy, love, and grace are His normal, usual work.

<u>Summary Points</u>

Warren Wiersbe concisely contrasts God's righteous anger with our natural propensity to sin when angry:

In the Garden, Peter was slow to hear, swift to speak, and swift to anger – and he almost killed a man with the sword. Many church fights are the result of short tempers and hasty words. There is a godly anger against sin (Eph. 4:26); and if we love the Lord, we must hate sin (Ps. 97:10). But man's anger does not produce God's righteousness (Jas. 1:20). In fact, anger is just the opposite of the patience God wants to produce in our lives as we mature in Christ (Jas. 1:3-4).[4]

From this scriptural evaluation of God's anger and His exhortations concerning our anger, the following practices should characterize our anger management:

1. I must be slow to anger.
2. I must be righteously provoked to anger.
3. My anger should develop before righteous action is taken.
4. My anger must have a present righteous purpose to prompt action.
5. If my anger cannot immediately serve righteousness, it must be released.
6. My anger is to be quickly relinquished after serving a just purpose.
7. God's work through wrath is not His usual, normal work.

Be Responsible

"Be responsible." It's a term that authority figures have been echoing in our ears since we were toddlers. God demands the same responsibility concerning the management of our anger. Every believer shall render an account of his or her behavior before the Judgment Seat of Christ.

But why dost thou judge thy brother? Or why dost thou set at nought thy brother? for we shall all stand before the judgment seat of Christ (Rom. 14:10).

For we must all appear before the judgment seat of Christ; that every one may receive the things done in his body, according to that he hath done, whether it be good or bad (2 Cor. 5:10).

The Judgment Seat of Christ is not a judgment of salvation but of the believer's deeds. Eternal salvation is obtained from God when an individual believes the gospel message (Jn. 5:24, Rom. 10:9). There is, however, a future day when all Christian behavior must be judged for reward or loss of reward (1 Cor. 3:11-15). Hidden motives will be revealed, and everything done for Christ and in His strength will be rewarded; all else will be burned up in judgment – and we will be glad to see it go! When the believer's anger is brought under the control of God to further righteousness, he or she has the opportunity to impact the kingdom of God presently and to savor the benefit throughout eternity as well.

As we live in a post-Christian society, it is vitally important that believers learn to properly control their angry feelings in order to be a good testimony of Jesus Christ. Our society is ravaged by the ills of sin, and immense potential for rage exists. We could easily be ruled by anger in response to a wicked world system characterized by pain, suffering and sin, if we chose to be. This, however, was not the practice of Christ, His apostles, or spirit-filled Christians down through the centuries. They understood that where there was no fear of the Lord, there would be social consequences. *"The fear of the Lord is the beginning of knowledge: but fools despise wisdom and instruction"* (Prov. 1:7). *"The fear of the Lord prolongeth days: but the years of the wicked shall be shortened* (Prov. 10:27).

Furthermore, believers are to be given to prayer, and Paul exhorts us to never approach the throne of grace with wrath in our hearts (The word for wrath is *orge*, which means resentment – 1 Tim. 2:8.). The self-promoting attitudes of the flesh are not to rule our prayer life!

It is true that neglect and physical and emotional abuse have induced deep-seated and unrelenting anger in the hearts of numerous children today, but even the worst of these will find their resolution at the cross of Jesus Christ. He offers each individual a new and living way. Without Christ, these children often grow up to be adults with a boiling pot of bitterness, wrath, and hate just waiting to spill over and scald anyone who slightly stirs them. Marriages commonly end in divorce, abuse escalates and hostile behavior is learned by the next generation so that the cycle continues. Scripture clearly identifies how the anger of others affects us negatively.

Make no friendship with an angry man; and with a furious man thou shalt not go (Prov. 22:24).

An angry man stirreth up strife, and a furious man aboundeth in transgression (Prov. 29:22).

A wrathful man stirreth up strife: but he that is slow to anger appeaseth strife (Prov. 15:18).

Regardless of the world's injustices and our past pain, what we do when we feel angry is our choice. We are completely responsible to God for the way we respond when angry and to others who are angry. Neither past hurts, enduring injustices, nor physical adversity are holy ground for inflicting others with unrighteous behavior. Despite the circumstances, a Christian should seek to secure a right response to the wrong behavior of others. The goal is to serve others by provoking them to a proper response – not to further incite them to greater sin.

The north wind driveth away rain: so doth an angry countenance a backbiting tongue (Prov. 25:23).

A soft answer turneth away wrath: but grievous words stir up anger (Prov. 15:1).

A gift in secret pacifieth anger: and a reward in the bosom strong wrath (Prov. 21:14).

So Jonathan arose from the table in fierce anger, and did eat no meat the second day of the month: for he was grieved for David, because his father had done him shame (1 Sam. 20:34).

By applying a proper response, we can aid others in ceasing from backbiting, wrath and other anger-motivated behaviors. King Saul was roused by jealousy to kill David, but Jonathan's righteous anger served David by aiding his escape and preserving his life. Likewise, we must use righteous anger to benefit and serve others. It is our stewardship to do so.

It has often been stated that you become like those you spend time with. It is true. *He that walketh with wise men shall be wise: but a companion of fools shall be destroyed* (Prov. 13:20). *Do not be misled: "Bad company corrupts good character* (1 Cor. 15:33 NIV). If you closely associate with an angry man – you will become angry (Prov. 22:24-25). The marks of a disciple of Christ are to learn the Master (Mt. 11:29) and to become like Him (Mt. 10:25). If you fellowship closely with Christ, you will become like the blessed Savior – you will learn His mind and gain His moral likeness (Phil. 2:1-5).

Although the Lord Jesus is rarely spoken of in Scripture as being angry, it is evident that His righteous anger flared on a number of occasions. The Lord glorified the Father when He made a scourge to drive the animals and their masters from the temple and threw over the tables of the moneychangers. These racketeers had turned the temple into a place of commerce and thievery, but the Lord restored it to a house of prayer (Mt. 21:12-13; Jn. 2:14-17). While angry with the Pharisees, the Lord healed a man on the Sabbath day to challenge their shallow spiritual existence (Mk. 3:5). With utter contempt, He later warned them of impending judgment (Mt. 23:13-36).

At other times, the Lord's anger did not result in direct action, instead He relinquished the matter into His Father's care. Herein the Lord demonstrated that there are times to defer from righteous anger. *The discretion of a man deferreth his anger; and it is his glory to pass over a transgression* (Prov. 19:11). It may not be the appropriate timing to address the matter, or you may decide that in the sight of eternity the grievance is too trivial to pursue. Might we follow the Lord's example at such times?

> *For what glory is it, if, when ye be buffeted for your faults, ye shall take it patiently? But if, when ye do well, and suffer for it, ye take it patiently, this is acceptable with God. For even hereunto were ye called: because Christ also suffered for us, leaving us an example, that ye should follow His steps: Who did no sin, neither was guile found in His mouth: Who, when He was reviled, reviled not again; when He suffered, He threatened not; but committed Himself to Him that judgeth righteously* (1 Pet. 2:20-23).

Christ offered intercession for the very wretches that had nailed Him to a tree, *"Father forgive* [suffer] *them; for they know not what they do"* (Lk. 23:34). Times will come when the child of God can do nothing but abdicate his or her lawful claim for justice before the throne of grace. God is not mocked, and His judgment shall be rendered in due time. In so doing, we mimic the self-sacrificing attitude of the beloved Savior who offered many such sweet-smelling sacrifices unto His Father (Eph. 5:2). In the same spiritual sense, we may also offer discreetly prepared sacrifices upon the golden altar of incense in the yonder realm of glory. At such times, before the eternal and immutable throne of heaven, a pillar of sweet aroma ascends into the very nostrils of God where He breathes it in and is refreshed at the remembrance of His own Son's selfless sacrifice. Christ alone is our altar (Heb. 13:10) and the only means by which our personal sacrifices are presented in heaven and appreciated by God the Father.

If you are finding it difficult for your anger to serve others, release the ill offense unto the Lord as a self-sacrifice and cease from being angry. The act of surrendering will cost you all your rights in the matter, but such a sacrifice is precious in God's sight. Remember, however, that once it is laid on God's altar of sacrifice, human folly dare not snatch it off again. Such an action would insult Christ's own selfless example and mock His gracious character. There is no such thing as a sacrifice unto the Lord which does not cost the offerer something (1 Chron. 21:24)!

Proper Anger Management

From the Lord's own flawless character and blameless behavior, we may conclude that two types of emotional responses characterize proper anger management: either a determination to serve God or a willingness to suffer loss and be a living sacrifice unto God. Service or sacrifice – these are the only two means in which our anger can glorify God.

In the first, the believer yields his or her body as an instrument of righteousness to accomplish a just and biblical response that will serve others and exalt God. The response may be one of instruction, exhortation, rebuke, or in extreme situations, physical intervention. Generally, a serving anger response will edify the offending party or intervene to alleviate the consequences of an unrighteous action. For this cause, we may provoke one another: *"And let us consider one another to provoke unto love and to good works"* (Heb. 10:24).

> He that would be angry and sin not must not be angry with anything but sin.
> – Thomas Secker

In the sacrificing response, the believer determines that it is better to suffer hurt and/or loss than to allow his or her anger to provoke a response. The entire matter (the offense and the retribution of the offender) is entrusted to the Lord. In so doing, the believer follows the example of the Savior and, thus, honors God!

Proper Anger in Leadership

Paul provides Titus with spiritual and moral qualifications for the activity of recognizing church leadership (elders). In Titus 1:7 we read, *"For a bishop must be blameless, as the steward of God; not self-willed, not soon angry, not given to wine, no striker, not given to filthy lucre."* A church leader is to be thick-skinned and not a man prone to violence. The qualification does not limit the elder from being angry, for certainly evil doings will arouse his anger, but it does ensure that he is one who demonstrates proper control when angry.

J. Oswald Sanders provides the following historical examples of men who were moved by righteous indignation for the glory of God.

Great leaders who have turned the tide in days of national and spiritual declension have been men who could get angry at the injustices and abuses that dishonor God and enslaved men. It was righteous anger against the heartless slave traders that caused Wilberforce to move heaven and earth for the emancipation of slaves. F.W. Robertson was similarly stirred by righteous anger on one occasion. Describing his reaction he said: "My blood was at the moment running fire, and I remembered that once in my life I had felt a terrible might; I knew and rejoiced to know that I was inflicting the sentence of a coward's and a liar's hell." Martin Luther claimed that he "never did anything well until his wrath was excited, and then he could do anything well."[1]

> Thou to wax fierce
> In the cause of the Lord!
> Anger and zeal
> And the joy of the brave,
> Who bade *thee* to feel,
> Sin's slave?

Unknown

Summary Points

1. Despite past abuse and oppression or present hardships and difficulties, we are completely responsible to God for our behavior. We have an anger stewardship, and in a future day, everyone will render an account to God of his or her behavior.

2. Anger serves God when its response is guided by Scripture and empowered by the Holy Spirit.

3. The Lord Jesus demonstrated two appropriate anger responses: to serve God or to release His anger as a sweet-smelling sacrifice to His Father.

4. "Anger" is only one letter from "danger;" be responsible!

Serving God or Our Flesh

With the testimony of Christ afresh in our minds, let us now investigate and contrast mankind's anger tendencies. The holy pages of Scripture record for our learning many examples of individuals who either allowed their anger to serve God or, unfortunately, allowed it to serve themselves.

Moses

While Moses was receiving the Law from God on Mt. Sinai, the children of Israel were below creating themselves a new god – the golden calf. God was furious over this offense and instructed Moses to immediately depart from the mount and return to camp. Exodus 32:19 recounts, *"And it came to pass, as soon as he came nigh unto the camp, that he saw the calf, and the dancing: and Moses' anger waxed hot, and he cast the tables out of his hands, and brake them beneath the mount."*

Moses had an honorable reason to be angry – the children of Israel had committed a grievous sin (idolatry) against the Lord. If he had brought the stone tablets in to the camp at that moment, swift and sure judgment would have been demanded and executed. Therefore, in this way, his anger served the people in that it offered them the possibility of repentance and restoration with God, rather than immediate and fierce judgment.

However, later in their desert pilgrimage, the constant murmuring of the Israelites motivated Moses to anger and, consequently, to rebel against God. In his anger, Moses struck the rock to obtain water instead of following God's instruction of speaking to the Rock. Moses' action broke the Old Testament "type" of Christ being the Rock, which was to be struck only once in picturing the Lord's complete sacrifice for sin at Calvary. After Calvary, God has bestowed blessings to His children through answering prayers directed to our Great High Priest, Jesus Christ (Heb. 4:14-16) and not through any further suffering of Christ for sin (Heb. 10:10-18). God punished Moses for this misuse of anger by not allowing him to lead the people into the Promised Land. Moses, a man who loved the Lord, had allowed his anger to elevate himself in the sight of the people and to diminish God's testimony before them (Num. 20:8-11). *"And the Lord spake unto Moses and Aaron, Because ye believed Me not, to sanctify Me in the eyes of the children of Israel, therefore ye shall not bring this congregation into the land which I have given them"* (Num 20:12). Moses was judged because his anger had sought his own glory and not God's.

King Saul

When Nahash the Ammonite threatened the inhabitants of Jabesh-gilead, Saul became angry and assembled Israel together to fight the Ammonites. *"And the Spirit of God came upon Saul when he heard those tidings, and his anger was kindled greatly"* (1 Sam. 11:6) is a good example of man's righteous anger being brought under Spirit-control to promptly serve others and to glorify God. His anger prompted a positive response that led to a great victory.

Later, however, his jealousy over David infuriated him to be unjust with his son Jonathan: *"Then Saul's anger was kindled against Jonathan, and he said unto him, Thou son of the perverse rebellious woman..."* (1 Sam. 20:30). Saul's anger

24

was so intensely reckless that he actually attempted to thrust a javelin through his own son. This is nothing less than manic rage.

King David

As a youth, David was provoked by strong emotions to fight Goliath in the name of the Lord God. Although the text does not specifically state that David was angry, his zeal for the Lord was provoked by Goliath's mockery of God. David was enabled by righteous anger to accomplish a spectacular feat – the slaying of a giant and the leading of Israel into triumph over the Philistines, the enemy of God's people (1 Sam. 17).

Years later when David was ruling over Israel as King, the prophet Nathan was sent by God to confront David concerning his sin of adultery with Bathsheba. As Nathan told David a story about a rich man seizing a poor man's only ewe lamb in order to serve a visitor, David became enraged: *"And David's anger was greatly kindled against the man; and he said to Nathan, As the Lord liveth, the man that hath done this thing shall surely die"* (2 Sam. 12:5). Nathan had used this story to express to David God's anger over his sin. David had abused the power of the throne upon which God had put him; thus, the consequence of judgment would be forthcoming.

David's anger in the former example served and promoted the glory of God, but his anger invoked by Nathan's rebuke was blind and hypocritical. It demonstrates how easy it is for anger to cloud rational thinking and logical conclusions. Being out of fellowship with his God, David had been miserable for nearly a year. Others may not know our secret sins, but both God and we know all about them. *"Be sure your sin will find you out"* (Num. 32:23). When we are not in communion with God, our anger has the greatest opportunity to be provoked and to pursue the most ungodly outworking. David's son Absalom harbored a deep hatred for his half-brother Amnon for having raped his sister Tamar – in time, Absalom's unresolved anger led to murder (2 Sam. 13:22-32).

The Older Son

In the parable of the "Prodigal Son" (Luke 15), the anger of the older son kept him from entering the same door of repentance that the remorseful younger son had entered to find forgiveness and full restoration with his father: *"And he was angry, and would not go in: therefore came his father out, and intreated him"* (Lk. 15:28). Given the reply of the older son to his father, it is evident that his anger was self-focused and self-serving. The Lord told this parable to rebuke the religious Jews of the day because through religious form they were close to God (as the older son was in the field near the house), but spiritually speaking they were dead (They would not repent as the younger son had.). Consequently, they were not experiencing the Father's joy or fellowship, which could only be obtained through a new life in Christ. Selfish anger often prohibits us from securing God's blessing because of its unyielding pride. *"When pride cometh, then cometh shame: but with the lowly is wisdom"* (Prov. 11:2). *"A man's pride shall bring him low: but honour shall uphold the humble in spirit"* (Prov. 29:23). If pride be present in our anger, our response will not work the righteousness of God – for God hates pride (Prov. 8:13)!

The Master Hosting a Great Supper

"So that servant came, and showed his Lord these things. Then the master of the house being angry said to his servant, Go out quickly into the streets and lanes of the city, and bring in hither the poor, and the maimed, and the halt, and the blind"

(Lk. 14:21). As a result of many refusing the invitation to the great supper (picturing the Jewish rejection of Christ), the opportunity for salvation went out to the Gentiles. There was righteous provocation to behave in this manner – the master's anger ultimately served as a wider blessing to more people while punishing those who had rejected his offer.

To Serve God or to Serve the Flesh?

As stated previously, anger is a powerful emotion, not a behavior. If applied properly, anger promotes the righteousness of God and will have a constructive benefit. If anger is allowed to stir up the flesh to hate, to strife, or to wrath (or other works of the flesh mentioned in Galatians 5), destructive behavior will be the result. The working of the flesh never upholds the righteousness of God (Rom. 8:8). Absolutely nothing that is inherent within our fallen and corrupt flesh can please God in and of itself: *"For I know that in me (that is, in my flesh) dwelleth no good thing; for to will is present with me, but how to perform that which is good I find not"* (Rom. 7:18).

Thus, the unbeliever suffers in sin with no hope of bringing his or her debased flesh into a God-honoring competence, but there is hope for those who have acknowledged their sinful condition before God and have accepted His only solution for their sin (the sacrificial death of His Son Jesus Christ). The Lord Jesus proclaimed:

> *I am the door: by Me if any man enter in, he shall be saved, and shall go in and out, and find pasture. The thief cometh not, but for to steal, and to kill, and to destroy: I am come that they might have life, and that they might have it more abundantly. I am the good shepherd: the good shepherd giveth His life for the sheep* (Jn. 10:9-11).

Christ was raised up from the dead that we might have a full and abundant life in Him. For this reason, God resides within a Christian after conversion (Gal. 2:20). Every believer is a new creation in Christ (2 Cor. 5:17) and becomes a temple of the living God (1 Cor. 6:19-20)! The desires of our depraved flesh, however, are still present within the believer, and this repulsive nature can only be controlled by the Holy Spirit. Therefore, the force of our anger, when righteously invoked, must be submitted to the will of God (obedient to the Word of God) and yielded to the Holy Spirit's control.

> *For the law of the Spirit of life in Christ Jesus hath made me free from the law of sin and death. For what the law could not do, in that it was weak through the flesh, God sending His own Son, in the likeness [appearance] of sinful flesh and for sin, condemned sin in the flesh, that the righteousness of the law might be fulfilled in us, who walk not after the flesh, but after the Spirit* (Rom. 8:2-4).

What might the consequences be if a believer does not allow the Holy Spirit to manage his or her anger? Despite all the fancy terms presently ascribed to anger, there are basically two ways to mishandle anger and, as we have learned, two means of properly managing anger for God's honor.

Mishandling Anger

Generally speaking, anger may be mishandled in two ways: it may be internalized or externalized. I internalize anger by swallowing it, instead of allowing it to accomplish a righteous cause, then extinguishing it. Internalizing or suppressing anger leads to **resentment**. Internalized anger is like leprosy – it will devour from the inside out over time. In this scenario, I will become easily irritated with and resentful of others but will rarely voice my feelings directly. Instead, I jab, gossip, dig, avoid, imagine evil and adopt guerrilla warfare tactics of discrete revenge. In the end, festering anger will adversely affect every relationship, including the believer's fellowship with God. In this self-imposed emotional state, my anger first afflicts me, then it harms others. Internalizing anger is like voluntarily locking yourself in a caliginous dungeon then feeling superior while you slowly watch yourself rot away.

The opposite of internalizing anger is to allow it to rule openly. Instead of letting anger work the righteousness of God, I choose to clutch its tail and be dragged down paths of aggressive and often brutal conduct. My speech is sharp, and my actions towards others are aggressive; at times, I am even explosive. I vent **rage** easily and often towards those I love the most. Consequently, I have damaged or severed most of my closest relationships. This realization is horrifying to me, for deep down I truly love those who no longer want to have any association with me. I am weary of my destructive behavior but am unsure of how to let go of the anger that now firmly grips me. Externalized anger is like being strapped to a wild bronco that ceases to kick and buck only when fatigue sets in, but which will invariably exhibit its unbroken and untamed spirit again.

David Dunlap produced the following table to contrast God's righteous indignation with man's unrighteous wrath.

God's Wrath (Indignation)	Man's Wrath
Controlled, with purpose	Uncontrolled, impatient
Without hatred	With hatred and revenge
Not selfish	Selfish
Often as an expression of concern	An expression of anger
Its goal is to limit/correct evil acts	Its goal is to harm or do damage
An expression of love	An expression of revenge
Against injustice	Against personal injury or attack
Against planned disobedience	Against those who oppose

Anger Flavors

The original language of the New Testament is much more "colorful" than is our English language. In reference to anger, a variety of closely related Greek words are employed to convey precise distinction or degrees of meaning. Consequently, the Greek text presents several "flavors" of anger. The Greek language clearly conveys that not all anger is bad. The following are the main Greek words used in the New Testament to speak of anger and their associated outcomes:

Rage – Thumos

Thumos (thoo-mos') is rendered "fierceness," "indignation," and most often "wrath." It speaks of <u>turbulent emotions and a boiling up of expression</u> – a sudden explosion. *Thumos* occurs eighteen times in the New Testament; ten of which appear in Revelation. Seven of the Revelation references speak of God's wrath, while everywhere else in the New Testament *thumos* has a negative meaning in relationship with faulty human behavior – **rage.** I call it **blowing up.**

Resentment – Orge

Orge (or-gay'), speaks of violent passion; by implication, punishment. It is rendered in KJV as "anger," "indignation," "vengeance," and "wrath." *Orge* occurs 36 times in the New Testament and has a long-lasting attitude that seeks revenge –

resentment. I refer to it as **clamming up**. Connected with *Orge* are two related words: *Orgizo*, occurring eight times in the New Testament, speaks of the act of developing a deep-seated and settled anger; *parorgizo*, used only twice in Scripture, is a strengthened form of *orge* meaning "to quiver with strong emotion."

W. E. Vine concisely contrasts and explains the meaning of *Thumos* and *Orge*:

> *Thumos*, "wrath" (not translated "anger"), is to be distinguished from *orge*, in this respect, that *thumos* indicates a more agitated condition of the feelings, an outburst of wrath from inward indignation, while *orge* suggests a more settled or abiding condition of mind, frequently with a view to taking revenge. *Orge* is less sudden in its rise than *thumos*, but more lasting in its nature.[1]

In general, *thumos* quickly blazes up (rage) then abruptly subsides; whereas, *orge* speaks more of a lingering agitated condition (resentment). Oswald Chambers saw the latter offense as being more destructive to relationships, "The man who loses his temper quickest is the one who finds it quickest. The man you need to beware of is not the man who flares up, but the man who smolders, who is vindictive and harbors vengeance."[2]

Indignation – Aganakteo

Aganakteo (ag-an-ak-teh'-o), from *agan* (much) and *achthos* (grief), means "to be greatly afflicted or displeased," or in the figurative sense, "indignant." It is directly translated as "indignation" four of the seven times it appears in the New Testament. The remaining three times the meaning of "being much displeased" is indicated. *Aganakteo* is **Indignation**. Through righteous provocation, this anger seeks to **lift God up**.

New Testament examples of *aganakteo*:

*But when Jesus saw it, **He was much displeased** [had indignation], and said unto them, Suffer the little children to come unto Me, and forbid them not: for of such is the kingdom of God* (Mk. 10:14).

*And when the ten heard it, **they were moved with indignation** against the two brethren* (Mt. 20:24).

From the Old Testament, we view the righteous indignation of the Lord against the wicked:

For the indignation of the Lord is upon all nations, and His fury upon all their armies: He hath utterly destroyed them, He hath delivered them to the slaughter (Isa. 34:2).

And the Lord rooted them out of their land in anger, and in wrath, and in great indignation, and cast them into another land, as it is this day (Deut. 29:28).

Stuart Briscoe accurately describes indignation:

The wrath of God is as pure as the holiness of God. When God is angry He is perfectly angry. When He is displeased there is every reason He should be. We tend to think of anger as sin; but sometimes it is sinful not to be angry. It is unthinkable that God would not be purely and perfectly angry with sin.[3]

So What May Anger Accomplish?

Anger can serve God or serve the flesh. From Scripture, we may derive four basic outlets in which anger will manifest itself. Two of these behaviors are positive and God-honoring, while the remaining two lead to sin. Two behaviors are Spirit-controlled and two are flesh-motivated.

Rage or "Blowing Up"

Rage is violent, an expression of uncontrolled anger – a work of the flesh with wrongdoing and harm visible. Dr. Les Carter refers to it as **"Open Aggression"** and defines it as "a self-preserving stand for personal worth, needs, and convictions at someone else's expense."[4] Rage doesn't think, it controls in order to satisfy selfish need. Balaam was so controlled by his anger that he was completely unaware he was conversing with a donkey (Num. 22:29).

Resentment or "Clamming Up"

Resentment represses feelings of anger, which then smolder and ultimately seek covert revenge. Often it is social etiquette that forces us to resolve expressions of rage and to choose resentment as a more acceptable form of expressing anger. Denying the existence of angry feelings and pushing them down inside creates resentment. This pattern inevitably leads to tension and a subtle but unyielding attack upon others. Dr. Les Carter refers to it as **"Passive Aggression,"** then notes "Like open aggression, anger expressed through passive aggression involves preserving personal worth, needs, and convictions at someone else's expense. But it differs in that it is accomplished in a quieter manner, causing less personal vulnerability."[5]

Indignation or "Lifting God Up"
Indignation sacrifices selfish interest in order to intensely and actively pattern God's own abhorrence of sin.

Release or "Giving Anger Up"
Release determines not to take revenge or corrective action but is determined to suffer loss and simply entrust the Lord with the outcome of the offense. It waits patiently for the opportunity to extend forgiveness when the offending party confesses sin (Lk. 17:3), but until such time the matter remains in the background of one's thinking (The matter is not allowed to rule one's thought life.).

The following table contrasts the goals and consequences of the before-mentioned anger-motivated behaviors.[6]

Anger-Motivated Behaviors

Rage:	Resentment:	Indignation:	Release:
Seeks to do wrong	Seeks to hide wrong	Seeks to correct wrong	Seeks to absorb the wrong
Seeks to destroy	Seeks to hurt	Seeks to oppose evil	Seeks to allow God to avenge
Seeks vengeance	Seeks to get even in time	Seeks justice	Seeks to allow God to judge
Open warfare	Guerilla warfare	Defends the truth	Prays for resolution
Guided by selfishness	Guided by cowardice	Guided by mercy	Guided by faith
Defends itself	Defends status quo	Defends God or others	Doesn't defend self
Prohibited in Bible	Prohibited in Bible	Required in Bible	Exemplified in Bible

In summary, all anger consciously or unconsciously chooses to serve God or self. Anger vented as blatant rage or clandestine resentment hurts others and us – which does not work the righteousness of God. Anger that is motivated by present righteous circumstances and that is controlled by the Spirit upholds the righteousness of God. Anger released to God as a selfless act of absorbing wrongdoing also upholds the righteousness of God. In such cases, we by faith, encourage God to display His glory through supernatural intervention.

Investigating the Cause of Anger

How long has it been since you were angry? What aroused your anger? For many, anger intrudes far too often into daily affairs. Stress, fatigue, hostile work environments, etc. continually test our spiritual resolve and emotional control. But why do I let situations bother me more some days than others? On Monday, I sail through the day nearly unmindful of the external tension, but on Wednesday – well, nobody better cross my path. Why the difference in behavior, given the same external situation?

To understand the cause of anger, we must first offer an important distinction of external and internal conditions. **External conditions** are those situations that adversely affect and frustrate us. Normally, we have little or no control over these afflicting circumstances. These external conditions can be generally categorized as four types of influences: loss, threats, frustration, or rejection. These external conditions generally stir up other emotions initially, for anger is not a primary emotion, but if **internal emotional conditions** exist within the individual, these external agencies urge angry feelings. Dr. Richard Walters writes:

> When our dominant internal conditions include guilt, a sense of helplessness (from low self-esteem or lack of support), unrealistic expectations (from excessive self-esteem or his-

tory of abuse of power), or aimlessness, the emotional response is likely to include anger, and it is probable that the angry individual will choose a destructive expression of it.[1]

If a Christian has a healthy self-acceptance in Christ and a mature understanding of God's purpose for his or her life, feelings of anger will not only be less but much more likely to terminate with righteous indignation or release than with rage and resentment.

Understanding External Conditions

Loss

The most common and most severe conditions of loss would be the death of a loved one, natural disasters which affect personal property, and accidents which result in incapacitating physical or mental faculties. Less severe feelings of loss might be associated with the "empty nest syndrome," loss of employment, or the termination of a life long goal before its realization. Thus, the primary feelings associated with these conditions would typically be pain, regret, sorrow, depression, and grief. These feelings are often so strong that angry feelings can be freely spawned if one determines that the condition was unjust, caused inconvenience, or shadowed the future with a cloud of anxiety. Of course nothing crosses the Lord's desk without being approved for His glory and our overall benefit. When these self-centered primary feelings resulting from loss seize control of our minds, anger will seek a target. Often the target will be those who have escaped the tragedy and are enjoying what the angered individual cannot.

Judges 14 and 15 records the marriage of Samson to a Philistine woman. After having lost the riddle wager, Samson deserted his wife and returned to his father's house. The woman's father then gave Samson's wife to another man. Later, when Samson returned for his wife, the woman's father would not permit Samson to secure her. Samson, feeling the loss of his wife, became enraged and sought revenge. Unfortunately, his rage targeted the Philistine people as a whole instead of the individuals that had wronged him. As a result, he burned their fields and slaughtered many of them. While it is true that God raised up Samson as a judge to deliver Israel from the Philistine oppression (Jud. 15:11), his response is a good example of "loss" fueling personal rage. The Philistines deserved judgment for their harsh treatment of God's people, and God used Samson's anger in a wider sense to punish them.

Threats

Threats are derived from a number of sources: competition in the workplace, economic woes, rampant immorality, a rising crime rate, war and rumors of war. As we have no control over these factors, it would be a natural response to fret over them. Feelings of anxiety, fear, helplessness and insecurity would tend to rule our thinking. The flesh seeks a target to vent these strong feelings upon, but often the person perceived responsible is untouchable, so the flesh picks a more localized target, like family and friends. Remembering that God is sovereign over creation will aid our thinking in blaming others for the conditions in which we live.

In Nehemiah 5, an unfortunate external situation threatened the incredible task of rebuilding the wall that had once encircled Jerusalem in such a way that many of those working on the wall felt threatened by economic peril. Times were hard, and many Jews had mortgaged off all their assets to feed their families. Now some parents were being forced to sell their children into servitude in order to survive. This dismal predicament was transforming a once harmonious workforce into one of hostile disunity. The wall construction project was in jeopardy of being suspended if the matter was not resolved quickly. Nehemiah *became "very angry"* when he learned of this situation. His righteous anger motivated him to rebuke the nobles and rulers among the people and to demand that these greedy men restore unto the people what had been imparted to them by God as an inheritance. His question *"Ought ye not to walk in the fear of our God?"* (Neh. 5:6) was a stinging reminder that their ultimate accountability for their conduct was to God.

Scripture instructs the believer to fear only God, not the animosity of men (Mt. 10:28). Satan is to be resisted, not feared (Jas. 4:7). Remembering whom we should and should not fear will assist us in focusing heavenward during distressing times. Judgment of all things shall come – everyone will have an accounting day before the Lord Jesus (Rom. 14:12). *"For the Father judgeth no man, but hath committed all judgment unto the Son. That all men should honor the Son, even as they honor the Father. He that honoreth not the Son honoreth not the Father which hath sent Him"* (Jn. 5:22-23).

Frustration and Disappointment

Frustration arises when we are prevented from obtaining a goal or a particular objective. We may have been passionately pursuing a lifetime objective only to run headlong into a roadblock or some effectual "dead end" over which we had no control. When old hopes return withered and unrealized, frustration occurs. Frustration may cause us to feel incompetent, inadequate, weak, or insignificant. If unchecked, these feelings can lead to unhealthy anger and, ultimately, an outburst of rage.

Please consider John's example. For five years, he had intensely sought a promotion at the company where he was employed. Shortly after learning that he had been denied this promotion again, he left the workplace only to get stuck in rush hour traffic. He was frustrated and felt helpless. Anger swelled up and demanded a target, so John blared his horn relentlessly at the other drivers. From his lowered window, he yelled obscenities at his fellow drivers, who were also ensnared by the same predicament. John had been stuck in traffic before but had previously not resorted to this base behavior. John's emotional state was such that external situations caused frustration. The work of frustration on his inner man was not properly resolved and produced unhealthy anger which then led to venting rage. John chose to direct his anger in an unhealthy way. He allowed himself to get infuriated and out of control. His obnoxious car horn could do nothing to improve the traffic situation or to obtain his promotion; in fact, his actions could only worsen the situation and damage his testimony.

Rejection

Rejection is a condition that most of us experience at an early age. No one appreciates being spurned or shunned. Perhaps you were excluded from a particular playground activity or game during grammar school recess, or possibly some social clique didn't recognize your existence, or maybe siblings ostracized you for being short, having freckles, etc. All of us have been insulted and had our dignity demoted. It is painful to feel unimportant and insignificant. We all have a deep need to be loved by others and to associate and communicate with our peers, family and friends.

In Genesis 4, Cain felt rejected by God because his offering of vegetables was not accepted. God then demonstrated His longsuffering nature by personally visiting and pleading with Cain to do what was right while reminding him of the consequences of rebellion, but his rejected feelings and wounded pride led to intense anger. His unrighteous anger needed a target to explode upon. It would have been extremely foolish to assault God with self-righteous vindication, so instead, Cain elected to murder his righteous brother Abel. Why? Because *"by faith Abel offered unto God a more excellent sacrifice than Cain"* (Heb. 11:4). God had accepted Abel but had rejected Cain.

Evaluation of Internal Conditions

External conditions may warrant righteous anger and godly action, but external conditions alone will not provoke unrighteous anger. External conditions are only a catalyst to ignite unrighteous anger if the right internal conditions exist within an individual. As a burning match has no power to ignite water-logged paper, such is a believer in right fellowship with God. When he or she is yielded to the power and control of the Holy Spirit and is full of Christ, the internal conditions that produce unrighteous anger will not be present when external situations batter the believer. It is difficult to incite rage or resentment from a believer resting in the Lord.

Hudson Taylor, a pioneer missionary to China in the mid-19th century, illustrated this fact to a younger fellow missionary through the following example. With the younger missionary looking on, Taylor bumped a full glass of water. After doing so, Taylor asked, "What came out of the glass when it was bumped?" The missionary responded, "water." Taylor then replied, "What came out of the glass when I bumped it is what was in it – the same is true of you. If you are full of Christ when you get bumped in life – Christ will come out, if you are full of the flesh – the flesh will come out."

> *Be not deceived; God is not mocked: for whatsoever a man soweth, that shall he also reap. For he that soweth to his flesh shall of the flesh reap corruption; but he that soweth to the Spirit shall of the Spirit reap life everlasting* (Gal. 6:7-8).

Internal conditions can be generally categorized into four classes: guilt, helplessness, unmet needs, and aimlessness. When confronted by external conditions, these conditions, if loitering in our inner man, may promote unrighteous anger.

Guilt

Guilt is the natural fallout of an offended human conscience. God wrote His moral law upon our hearts and integrated an internal protection system, called a conscience, to monitor it (Rom. 2:15); thus, we instinctively know right and wrong. *"Therefore to him that knoweth to do good, and doeth it not, to him it is sin"* (Jas. 4:17). Studying God's Word sharpens the conscience of the believer and enables him or her to more quickly identify and avoid behavior that offends God. The apostle Paul logically concluded in Romans 2 that every individual proves to themselves that they are indeed "sinners" because they feel guilty after violating their own conscience. Therefore, even with their best efforts, they could not continue in "well doing." Thus, guilt has its roots in original sin and can only be cleansed away by the blood of the Lord Jesus (Heb. 9:11-15).

Though the external condition of rejection perhaps triggered Cain's rage towards Abel, the internal condition was certainly one of guilt. Cain had rejected God's order and specific worship instructions. His God-bestowed moral alarm system, his conscience, was clanging with guilt. With pride at the helm and an offended conscience inflicting strong feelings of guilt, Cain's rage was easily triggered by what he surmised as being nothing less than rejection by His Creator. Yet, the Creator was not rejecting Cain but *"the way of Cain"* (Jude 11). It is God, not Cain, who determines man's rightful approach and mode of acceptable worship.

Helplessness

For the Christian, a sense of helplessness may result from feelings of low self-worth (in relationship to others) or of poor self-acceptance (in respect to how God created them), or from a general lack of emotional and physical support by others. We adopt a self-defeating mindset and, thus, cripple our minds with thoughts of being defenseless, powerless and incompetent. Often the fear of rejection by others and lack of nurturing friendships go hand in hand. Consequently, when calamity does strike, feelings of loneliness and isolation overwhelm those already feeling helpless.

Jacob had been tricked into marrying the wrong woman, Leah – Rachel's sister. Because he loved Rachel, he agreed to labor seven more years for Laban so that he might marry her also. Polygamy, especially where two sisters are involved, will naturally create a hostile home environment as both wives compete for their husband's affection. In this ancient culture, the ability to bear children was the most honorable gift of a wife to her husband. Children were a heritage of future blessing. Because Leah was despised, God opened her womb – because Jacob favored Rachel, God rendered her barren. One day Rachel could tolerate her bewildering situation no more.

And when Rachel saw that she bare Jacob no children, Ra-
chel envied her sister; and said unto Jacob, Give me chil-

dren, or else I die. And Jacob's anger was kindled against Rachel: and he said, Am I in God's stead, who hath withheld from thee the fruit of the womb? And she said, Behold my maid Bilhah, go in unto her; and she shall bear upon my knees, that I may also have children by her (Gen. 30:1-3).

Rachel felt helpless. The frustration of seeing Leah bear several sons in quick succession was overwhelming. Perhaps she rationalized a scenario of foul play or unfairness in the matter. Conceivably, a general sense of loss also triggered her charge against Jacob. Notice that Jacob reciprocated with anger towards Rachel for accusing him of wrongdoing. He likewise was feeling helpless in this matter and lashed back at Rachel, who in turn demanded that Jacob receive her handmaiden as a concubine. Desperate and helpless, Rachel sought children for Jacob through her handmaiden.

Unmet Needs or Expectations

This condition may result when a person is high on self or has tendencies to be controlling and abuse authority. This behavior is often ignorantly taught to toddlers by their parents. If parents reward their toddler for throwing a temper tantrum instead of training the child (either by allowing the child to afflict themselves in isolation or by applying the rod of reproof to the seat of learning), they unfortunately teach the child that "if you scream loud enough you will always get your way." A self-exalting and self-seeking behavior torments everyone. As this child embarks on puberty, the consequences of this learned behavior will affect every relationship the child has. During adolescence, emotions are heightened by hormonal changes; intense peer pressure exists, and the need for social acceptance is great. Angry outbursts erupt readily when self-expectations are not being met. The heavy-handed tactics used to manipulate others and the consequences of rage when the domination of others is not obtained often causes individuals to flee close association with this type of person.

When the Israelites were on the brink of entering Canaan, a Moabite king named Balak determined to impede their invasion by having their local pagan prophet Balaam curse them. Balak brought Balaam to three different high places overlooking the Israelite camp, offered burnt sacrifices to God, then asked Balaam to pronounce the curse. Yet, the Lord had a different idea, and each time the Spirit of God seized control of Balaam's vocal cords to utter a blessing upon the Israelites. *"And Balak's anger was kindled against Balaam, and he smote his hands together: and Balak said unto Balaam, I called thee to curse mine enemies, and, behold, thou hast altogether blessed them these three times"* (Num. 24:10). Balak was seeking an unrealistic expectation, an impossible outcome, and he knew it. How could God, who had delivered the Israelites from bondage and from Egypt, who had protected and nurtured them for 40 years in the desert, now curse His own people because wicked Balak had offered a few burnt offerings? After the third attempt to curse God's people failed, Balak's frustration provoked his verbal assault of Balaam.

Futile Existence or Aimlessness

This is a condition resulting from having no sound foundation in life. Those who have no real understanding of the meaning of life or purpose for their existence will naturally have feelings of aimlessness and futility. As there is no purpose in life or value apart from knowing and serving Christ, the unbeliever will naturally have this internal condition in the deepest part of his or her being.

We again examine Cain as a good example of aimlessness. After Cain had murdered his righteous brother Abel, God sought Cain out.

> *And He said, What hast thou done? The voice of thy brother's blood crieth unto Me from the ground. And now art thou cursed from the earth, which hath opened her mouth to receive thy brother's blood from thy hand; When thou tillest the ground, it shall not henceforth yield unto thee her strength; a fugitive and a vagabond shalt thou be in the earth. And Cain said unto the Lord, My punishment is greater than I can bear. Behold, Thou hast driven me out this day from the face of the earth; and from Thy face shall I be hid; and I shall be a fugitive and a vagabond in the earth; and it shall come to pass, that every one that findeth me shall slay me. And the Lord said unto him, Therefore whosoever slayeth Cain, vengeance shall be taken on him sevenfold. And the Lord set a mark upon Cain, lest any finding him should kill him. And Cain went out from the presence of the Lord, and dwelt in the land of Nod, on the east of Eden* (Gen. 4:10-16).

As a result of Cain's murderous rage, God drove Cain from His presence. Cain was destined to wander in the land of Nod (meaning "wandering"). This characterizes our life apart from knowing Christ. Note the contrast in accomplishments between the genealogies of Cain (Gen. 4) and the godly line of Seth (Gen. 5). Cain's line represents the outcome of an angry rebellious spirit living apart from God – an aimless existence in the world. Cain's descendants built cities (a society apart from God), domesticated cattle, were skilled musicians and craftsmen, and committed social crimes against one another. Cain's aimless condition and deep-seated anger passed down through the generations. Under the influence of Satan, Cain's descendants sought self-significance and independence from God through industry, commerce, science, and the arts. These things are not inherently wicked, but in the absence of God, possessions, careers, and abilities become idols and poor substitutes for communion with our Creator.

Cain's descendants are not mentioned as living or even dying. In the sight of eternity, their lives did not count for anything. It was as if they had never lived for their lives persisted outside the will and blessing of God. They lived for the day and were "earthly" in focus – an aimless spiritual existence that provides a deep-seated internal condition for anger to be triggered easily. In contrast, Seth's line lived for God and walked with God. Genesis 5 records that Seth's ancestors obeyed God in populating the earth with godly children. They simply lived and died and walked with God – their lives counted for eternity.

Summary

We can do little to alleviate external conditions in a world cursed by God and ruled by the *"prince of the power of the air"* (Eph. 2:2). However, we can take full responsibility for removing the internal conditions that cause us to unnecessarily fret and fume. Consider the air pressure within a balloon as representing internal conditions, while a pin symbolizes external conditions which we have little or no control over. If the balloon hangs limp with no internalized pressure, you can jab it all day with a pin, and it will not pop. This represents an individual who is rightly and spiritually dealing with internal conditions. If we are somewhat successful at alleviating internal pressure but choose to hold in certain others, the balloon begins to inflate. Yet, a balloon partially inflated can still withstand many pinpricks before visible ramifications are noticed (namely spewing or exploding). For those who choose not to properly confront internal conditions, the balloon rapidly fills, expands, and stretches to the point that any minor abrasion will cause an emotional outburst. By removing or managing internal conditions, the stored emotional pressure within us is released (vented safely), and we are able to withstand external offenses better without responding inappropriately. Therefore, the questions before us are, How do I remove pressurizing mindsets? and How can I learn to safely vent stored up emotional energy?.

Learning Christ

Ideally, a limp balloon should characterize the believer's life, but on this side of glory, Christ-likeness is pursued and not obtained (Phil. 3:10-12). Practically speaking, we all are prone to swell with internal pressure from time to time, some more than others. Also, some of us practice pressure release more safely than others.

It is at this point that the reader is best served by knowing the general solution to managing anger before investigating the "how to" aspects of controlling it. It is not "how to" but "whom to" that is crucial. Learning the person of Christ will radically diminish our angry feelings, bring security to our natural impulses of expression and guide righteous behavior when angry. The answer to the very question the Savior asked of others, *"What think ye of Christ?"* (Mt. 22:42), is also the key to properly controlling one's anger.

As we increase in our knowledge of Christ and rely more upon His grace, we are transformed to become more like Him. Adam forfeited God-likeness in Eden through sin, but through Christ's obedience, the believer has the present opportunity to regain it. In Peter's second epistle, he clearly links the knowledge of Christ with spiritual fruit bearing: *"For if these things* [faith, virtue, knowledge, self-control, patience, godliness, brotherly love, and love (from 2 Pet. 1:5-7)] *be in you, and abound, they make you that ye shall neither be barren nor un-*

fruitful in the knowledge of our Lord Jesus Christ" (2 Pet. 1:8). *"But grow in grace, and in the knowledge of our Lord and Savior Jesus Christ"* (2 Pet. 3:18). Concerning the latter verse, William MacDonald offers the following comments:

> There must be a twofold growth – in grace and in knowledge. Grace is the practical demonstration of the fruit of the Spirit. Growth in grace is not increased head knowledge or tireless activity; it is increasing likeness to the Lord Jesus. Knowledge means acquaintance with the Lord through the Word. Growth in knowledge means increasing study of the subjection to His words, works and ways.[1]

In fact, five times in his second epistle, Peter refers to directly knowing Christ as the means of spiritual fruitfulness or to not knowing Christ as the cause of spiritual deadness. In these exhortations, the Greek word for knowledge is *epignosis*, which means "to have full discernment of." But how is it possible to have full discernment of Christ – to intimately know Him thoroughly?

The apostle John poses a notable hyperbole at the conclusion of his account of the Lord's ministry on earth: *"And there are also many other things which Jesus did, which if they should be written every one, I suppose that even the world itself could not contain the books that should be written"* (Jn. 21:25). Paul also informs us it will require eternity to learn of *"the exceeding riches of His grace"* (Eph. 2:7). Therefore, we understand that there is more of Christ to learn than what has been revealed to us in God's Word or what we can comprehend now, but we must endeavor to learn what we can of Him now. *"The secret things belong unto the Lord our God: but those things which are revealed belong unto us and to our children for ever, that we may do all the words of this law"* (Deut. 29:29). As we learn Christ, our spiritual appetites are enhanced to know Him more. Through our obedience to revealed truth, Christ promises to manifest Himself to us more deeply (Jn. 14:21).

This is the passion of every true disciple of Christ – to know the Savior and to be like Him (Mt. 10:25, 11:29). The reality of spiritual fruitfulness is found in knowing Christ, learning His mind, practicing His presence, abiding with Him and relying on His infinite grace in times of need and for daily living. Dear believer, if you pursue Christ in this way, you will find that your anger tendencies will diminish and that you will gain much more spiritual control of your righteous anger when God's glory demands it. The balloon will remain limp for God's power will simply pass from you unhindered to accomplish His glory in the external situation that demands action. In effect, a massive flow of grace from your vessel, without pressure buildup, is realized. In this way, you secure the peace of God in your life.

The apostle Paul spoke of two kinds of peace in the believer's life. First of all, he spoke of the "peace with God": *"Therefore, being justified by faith, we have peace with God through our Lord Jesus Christ"* (Rom. 5:1). Because God's anger over all human sin was judicially satisfied by the substitutional death of Christ (1 Jn. 2:2), God can enter into a peaceful relationship with an individual who confesses their sinful state before God and exercises personal faith in trusting Christ as their Savior.

> *For when we were yet without strength, in due time Christ died for the ungodly. For scarcely for a righteous man will one die: yet peradventure for a good man some would even dare to die. But God commendeth His love toward us, in that, while we were yet sinners, Christ died for us. Much*

more then, being now justified by His blood, we shall be saved from wrath through Him. (Rom. 5:6-9).

The Greek word *eirene* (i-ray'-nay) is translated "peace" 88 out of 91 times it appears in the KJV New Testament. *Eirene* means to "bond together" or "be made at one again." It is literally translated in Acts 7:26 when Stephen recounts the historical efforts of Moses to restore two fighting Hebrews to peace; he sought to make them *"at one again."* He wanted peace and unity to exist between them, and this would only be accomplished when they were of one heart and mind. Through Christ, the repentant sinner has been made one again with God in relationship; thus, eternal salvation of the soul is in view. Yet, beyond this peace, there is another that God implores us to gain in our lives – "the peace of God."

Paul spoke of this peace when writing to the church at Philippi:

Rejoice in the Lord always: and again I say, rejoice. Let your moderation be known unto all men. The Lord is at hand. Be careful for nothing; but in every thing by prayer and supplication with thanksgiving let your requests be made known unto God. And <u>the peace of God</u>, which passeth all understanding, shall keep your hearts and minds through Christ Jesus (Phil. 4:4-7).

This is not salvation of the soul but of the mind. When we are one with God in our thinking, affections, attitudes, actions, and yes, even our anger, God's peace will then flood our souls. Therefore, the next time you are feeling anxious ask yourself, "In what area of my life am I not one with God in my thinking?" Learning Christ ushers peace into our lives and will drastically reduce our angry feelings to only those that God would have if He were in our shoes.

When the Lord Jesus first appeared to His disciples collectively on resurrection day, the first words from His lips were *"Peace be unto you"* (Jn. 20:19). Yet, in the verse 21, He repeats the exact same expression with adjoining instruction, *"Peace be unto you; as My Father hath sent Me, even so send I you."* Why did the Lord Jesus duplicate His own words? He was acknowledging that only through Him could one obtain peace with God, and no less only through Him would divine peace be acquired to practically represent Him in the world. If the unsaved are going to be brought to Christ, they must see Christ's peace within our lives and not uncontrolled anger. We must know Him and abide with Him to experience His peace. It is longing for His presence and knowing His presence. Do you know the presence and peace of Christ?

Hudson Taylor was once asked by an undergraduate student at a training conference, "Are you always conscious of abiding in Christ?" "While sleeping last night," he replied, "did I cease to abide in your house because I was unconscious of the fact? We should never be conscious of not abiding in Christ." When asked how he could speak to so many different meetings, Taylor responded, "Every morning I feed upon the Word of God, then I pass on through the day messages that have first helped me in my own soul."[2]

David Livingstone, a contemporary of Hudson Taylor, was divinely called to bring the gospel message to the interior of Africa, a field of harvest into which no other white man dared venture. For decades, he hazarded his life by exploring the perilous jungles of Africa and did so while suffering from acute malaria. Before dying, he had successfully trekked some 30,000 to 40,000 miles through the interior of Africa, all the time preaching the gospel of Jesus Christ to natives, many of whom were cannibals, and mapping the interior of Africa. He had hoped that his explorations and careful documentation would establish trade routes that would aid in abolishing the slave trade.

After these years of adversity, he was found dead in the simplest of living conditions: a grass hut with a bed, desk and chair. His body was recovered and brought back to England, where, at Westminster Abbey, an enormous funeral service was held and all of England honored this brave missionary. Livingstone's Bible was found alongside his body and examination of it found that the ink was nearly worn off of Psalm 46. Twice in that psalm we read, *"The Lord of hosts is with us; the God of Jacob is our refuge."* *"God is our refuge and strength, a very present help in trouble!"* Livingstone had etched his own record of trust upon the holy page by passing his finger repeatedly over text. What was it that had brought Him peace in the midst of danger and unforeseen trials that had constantly challenged his resolve? Knowing the presence and peace of Christ.

The Lord never forces Himself upon us, even when we are in distress. We must want Him for He has already promised to be with us. *"I will never leave thee, nor forsake thee"* (Heb. 13:5). *"Him that cometh to Me I will in no wise cast out"* (Jn. 6:37). During a life-threatening storm Jesus' disciples desperately rowed all night to cross the Sea of Galilee, but to no avail. Just when all hope was lost, the Lord Jesus was seen walking towards them upon the raging sea. Mark's gospel account states plainly that Jesus *"made as if He would go on"* (Mk. 6:48). When the disciples cried out to Him for help, however, He was more than willing to assist them. What comforting words He uttered to them, *"It is I; be not afraid."* What is there to fear while in Christ's presence? After expounding the Old Testament Scripture to the two disciples on the Emmaus Road, the Lord Jesus again demonstrated the same meekness:

> *And beginning at Moses and all the prophets, He expounded unto them in all the Scriptures the things concerning Himself. And they drew nigh unto the village, whither they went: and He made as though He would have gone further. But they constrained Him, saying, Abide with us: for it is toward evening, and the day is far spent. And He went in to tarry with them* (Lk. 24:27-29).

The Lord is not some ogre that forces people to seek Him and obtain His help, but for those who desire His presence and to know and trust Him, He will bestow peace beyond anything this world can boast. *"Thou wilt keep him in perfect peace, whose mind is stayed on Thee, because he trusteth Thee"* (Is. 26:3). Intimately knowing Christ will be the guard of peace that protects your heart from ungodliness. One of the ministries of the Holy Spirit is to ensure we both know and are conscious of the Lord Jesus Christ (Jn. 16:13-14). You will indeed find it difficult to be unjustly angry if you are full of Christ!

Knowing Christ and understanding His provision for the abundant life will assist the believer in anger management. Every Christian should:

1. Have a healthy self-acceptance (not self-esteem, but Christ-esteem) of who he or she is in Christ (Eph. 1:6).
2. Trust God's working in his or her life (Rom. 8:28).
3. Understand God's purpose for living (Rev. 4:11, Eph. 2:10).
4. Have a reverential fear of God (Mt. 10:28, Jas. 4:7).
5. Desire to intimately know Christ and be like Him (2 Pet. 1:8).

These fundamental tenets of Christian conduct will serve to minimize general feelings of anger. When such anger is conceived, it will be much more likely to terminate with righteous indignation or release than with rage and resentment. To learn Christ is the mysterious transforming way of God for the believer. Before the reader embarks on the "how to's" of anger management, he or she is first encouraged to get alone with Christ for an extended period of time. Spend an entire day fasting, confessing sin, praying, and reading Scripture which directly speaks of the Savior, and you will experience the transforming power of the Holy Spirit renew your love for Christ and strengthen your devotion to serve Him. One of the main ministries of the Holy Spirit is to teach us Christ – *"He shall glorify Me"* (Jn. 16:14).

Someday soon, our spiritual armor will abruptly fall to the ground with a clang; those pupils in the Lord's school will graduate, and all our tears will be wiped away by the Lord Himself. In a moment, a twinkling of an eye, every born again believer will be ushered into the glorious presence of the Lord Jesus – and we will be instantly like Him (Phil. 3:21)! No angry bents will complicate our thinking in His company. No bitterness will seek revenge. No hidden malice will vex our conscience ever again. No ranting, fuming, nor any unrighteous behavior or thinking will be found in heaven – only that which is pleasing to God. O Lord Jesus, come quickly!

> And is it so – I shall be like Thy Son?
> Is this the grace which He for me has won?
> Father of glory, (thought beyond all thought!),
> In glory, to His own blest likeness brought!

> J. N. Darby

Breaking the Anger Cycle

Knowing and abiding in Christ is the true secret to spiritual fruit bearing, yet it requires a concerted effort to learn Christ and to lay hold of Christ-likeness. In this pursuit, we also must labor to crucify (put to death) the natural desires of the flesh. In this cause, Scripture applies numerous exhortations and much practical guidance. A Spirit-controlled behavior will replace an anger-stimulated behavior. Generally speaking, if a new bent can be established with great regularity, it will become the new behavior in a few weeks. This, of course, depends on how deeply-seated the wrong behavior is, the level of accountability sought, and how intensely one truly aspires to establish the godly bent.

The following four-part remedy is suggested for correcting wrong anger behavior:

1. **First-aid Treatment** – provides initial stability to angry feelings.
2. **Deflate the Balloon** – reduces tension, eases stress, and channels internal energy productively.
3. **Don't Inflate the Balloon** – resolves internal conditions; this requires displacing un-Christ-like attitudes with God-honoring ones.
4. **Don't Jab the Balloon** – minimizes (where possible) agitating circumstances (external conditions) that prick, jab, and provoke us to anger.

First-aid will provide temporary relief of the anger tendencies. After first-aid has been applied, the next exercise is to reduce stress and to resolve self-imposed and self-inflicting internal conditions that are causing emotional imbalance. We must also rethink attitudes and motives and develop unselfish and Christ-centered thinking.

The final step to anger management is to minimize the circumstances that cause us to become angry. We must objectively review the taunting environments or irritating individuals that easily provoke us to anger and avoid them until such a time as we have learned proper control. A lot of sin could be circumvented if we simply removed ourselves from vulnerable situations.

First-aid Techniques

The purpose of first-aid is to bring temporary relief to one's initial angry feelings, thus, preventing the "fight and flight" or "hit and run" routine. For many individuals who tend to abruptly spew rage, a sense of guilt and remorse quickly follows their outburst. An apology is often offered within a few minutes of the event. Instead of immediately uttering unlovely words when an external condition arouses anger, "first-aid" seeks to stabilize the anger until it can be rightly evaluated, prioritized, and brought under the Holy Spirit's control. The goal is to break the anger cycle by allowing God and not our flesh to control our behavior.

Through first-aid, one learns to curb the initial impulses of anger. We want to be able to control our impulses rather than to allow them to control us. It is amazing what 10 to 15 seconds of silent resolution can accomplish to this end. Perhaps the reader has actually witnessed someone counting aloud from one to ten in order to prevent a vocalization of his or her frustrations. Most unrighteous anger is expressed immediately after some unexpected and irritating event (an external condition). Two millennia ago, Lucius Annaeus Seneca wrote, "The greatest remedy for anger is delay."[1]

If a short waiting period is imposed before responding to a provoking incident, the destructive force of the tongue and the violent tendency of our members will be better brought under control. Words will be fewer and less pungent, while actions will be more tempered and less aggressive. Initially self-treating our anger feelings will stabilize our "first response." Dr. Richard Walters writes:

> First-aid techniques are helpful first steps in learning to resolve angry feelings. These are simple methods to get quick physical and emotional relief and to help us keep our behavior under control so we don't make things worse. They pave the way for doing something constructive about the causes of anger. Many people will practice first-aid, feel better as a result, and then decide that everything is all right and therefore they don't need to express anger. However, first-aid is not enough by itself, because it does not produce lasting results.[2]

A paramedic who arrives on the scene of a terrible automobile accident will apply first-aid to initially treat the injured parties, so they can be transported to a hospital where complete and long-term medical care can be provided. First-aid stabilizes the injured but, in general, is not sufficient to cure the inherent medical emergency. Concerning anger, the long-term solution is attained by relieving internal tension, transforming wrong attitudes and minimizing the circumstances that cause anger to be aroused.

Applying Anger First-aid

Seeing and seeking God in every situation.

Acknowledging God's sovereign control of and rule over your life is critical. If there were no God, we would be a people most miserable for our suffering would serve no fruitful purpose and there would be no hope that our misery was working some greater good. *"And we know that all things work together for good to them that love God, to them who are the called according to His purpose"* (Rom. 8:28). Nothing happens in life that does not first obtain the Lord's approval. Scripture states *"that all things work together for good."* "All" means "all" – no exceptions. Our first thought in times of trouble ought to be "Lord, You allowed this to happen for a reason – do what You will – I will trust and rejoice in You."

For Hudson Taylor, this realization brought God's peace during a time of immense sorrow and loneliness. While serving in China, three of his seven children had died. Shortly, after sending the remaining four children back to England, Taylor's wife Maria also died. All his family was gone, and he was now alone in a foreign land. Taylor wrote the following at this juncture in his life:

> From my inmost soul I delight in the knowledge that God does or deliberately permits all things and causes all things to work together for good to those who love Him (Rom. 8:28). ... I saw that **it was good** for the Lord to take her, **good indeed for her**, and in His love He took her painlessly; and **not less good for me** who must henceforth toil and suffer alone – yet not alone, for God is nearer to me than ever. And now I have to tell Him all my sorrows and difficulties, as I used to tell dear Maria.[3]

Like Hudson Taylor, King David learned of God's sovereign control and of His peace during one of the most desperate times of his life. David and his loyal subjects had abandoned the palace at Jerusalem and had fled into the wilderness to escape a life-threatening rebellion led by his own son Absalom. Ahithophel, David's trusted counselor and friend, had betrayed him also. At this time, David is described as being weary, discouraged and weak-handed (2 Sam. 17:2). Although the author of 2 Samuel provides the historical narrative, but it is the Psalms that afford us the deeper sense of David's aching heart.

During this depressing time, David likely wrote Psalm 3, 61, and 63. In Psalm 61, David appears to be downcast, but while fleeing eastward through the wilderness, he notices a high rock. He was compelled to look up to gaze at the full stature of the rock. He thought this rock would suffice as a tower from which to spot the approaching enemy and as a natural shelter for the people. While contemplating this rock, the Spirit of God caused David to gaze beyond the insignificant to the tangible, higher, and mightier Rock – the Lord Himself. David was downcast, but the Lord lifted up his head that he might behold God in the situation: *"But Thou, O Lord, art a shield for me; my glory, and the lifter up of mine head"* (Ps. 3:3). Can you identify with David? Have you ever felt dejected, unloved, and betrayed by those who you love the most? David resolved his pain by acknowledging God's sovereignty in the matter and God Himself as his only strength and protection:

> *Hear my cry, O God; attend unto my prayer. From the end of the earth will I cry unto Thee, when my heart is overwhelmed: lead me to the rock that is higher than I. For Thou hast been a shelter for me, and a strong tower from the enemy. I will abide in Thy tabernacle forever: I will trust in the covert of Thy wings* (Ps. 61:1-4).

Dear believer, whatever difficulty you are trudging through, God is the lifter of your head. It will, however, require faith to lift up your eyes and to see Him in the situation. He is there, nonetheless, but you will not have hope in trials until you venture to gaze upward and know His presence. *"If we believe not...he abideth faithful"* (2 Tim. 2:13). He is faithful even when we are not – trust Him. Cry out for deliverance, shelter, and protection, and He will lift you up upon eagle's wings and hold you securely under them. Acknowledge His rule for your life, and you will have an "uplook" in life instead of a depressed "outlook." Lift your eyes to the higher Rock – the exalted Son of God, Jesus Christ.

Charles Spurgeon wrote the following concerning the security of the believer in God's hands:

> God our Father is here, and will be here all through the lonely hours; He is an almighty Watcher, a sleepless Guardian, a faithful Friend. Nothing can happen without His direction, for even hell itself is under His control. Darkness is not dark to Him. He has promised to be a wall of fire around His people – and who can break through such a barrier? Worldlings may well be afraid, for they have an angry God above them, a guilty conscience within them, and a yawning hell beneath them; but we who rest in Jesus are saved from all these through rich mercy.[4]

Stop, drop and pray.

We were taught as children that, if ever our clothing caught fire, we were to "stop, drop, and roll" to extinguish the flames. The reader may find this modified motto, "stop, drop and pray," helpful to circumvent initial urges to vent anger. The goal is to extinguish rage tendencies before someone else gets burned. Prayer demonstrates trust in the Lord and halts initial wrong behavior we will regret later. We are seeking to replace a bad behavioral bent with a good one. As soon as you become aware of angry feelings, resort to immediate prayer to effectively thwart rage tendencies.

Prayer is transforming. Have you ever sought the throne of grace while angry? It is disquieting to your soul to converse with God when you are angry. At first, your anger is evident, but as you begin to pray for the person that has hurt you, your heart is softened, and your aggression shifts to genuine remorse. You may begin contemplating how the offending parting has injured others, hurt themselves, or possibly defamed Christ through a poor testimony to the unsaved. "Stop, drop and pray" the next time you become angry – it really works, for it is impossible to stay angry long if engaged in righteous prayer. Prayer will transform our heart's disposition from anger to peace and from anguish to sympathy. Like Job, we will experience healing when we pray for those who have offended us (Job 42:10). Oswald Chambers provides helpful insight into the real purpose for praying:

> The point of prayer is not to get answers from God, but to have perfect and complete oneness with Him. If we pray only because we want answers, we will become irritated and angry with God. We receive an answer every time we pray, but it does not always come in the way we expect, and our spiritual irritation shows our refusal to identify ourselves truly with our Lord in prayer. We are not here to prove that God answers prayer, but to be living trophies of God's grace.[5]

Displace angry thoughts with spiritual ones.

When you first begin feeling angry, resort to quoting a key verse of Scripture or a spiritual poem that you have found helpful in convicting you of your anger bent in the past or perhaps humming a hymn or spiritual song. Strive to fill your mind with Christ – *"for out of the abundance of the heart the mouth speaks"* (Mt. 12:34). If you are thinking upon Christ, you will find it difficult to be un-Christ-like. It is not enough to just not think about the situation that is stirring up your anger; you must replace the thought with an appropriate one. Paul exhorts believers, *"Casting down imaginations, and every high thing that exalteth itself against the knowledge of God, and bringing into captivity every thought to the obedience of Christ"* (2 Cor. 10:5). To not respond aggressively to another who has affronted you requires personal resolve to glorify Christ and not yourself in the situation. If the believer understands his or her position and security in Christ, few personal insults, if any, will provoke an angry response.

Measure the issue.

While angry, we occasionally try to prove to ourselves that we are inherently capable of rendering proper behavioral choices. Have you witnessed someone, who a moment earlier was ranting and raving, suddenly adopt a sober tone of voice to answer a phone call that interrupted the theatrical expression? Deep down, we express unrighteous anger because it feels good to be angry because it satisfies some debased need of our flesh.

It is acceptable to raise one's voice to be heard but not for the purpose of conferring merit to words. I may shout a warning to one of my children if I determine that there is imminent danger, but I should never raise my voice in anger while addressing them or to authenticate my instructions. Husbands and wives should adopt the ground rule that yelling at each other is an unacceptable means of communication. The marriage union is to mimic the spiritual oneness of Christ and the Church. Does Christ ever yell at the Church? No, in fact Scripture only records the Lord Jesus crying out with a loud voice three times: once to be heard at the tomb of Lazarus and twice in His declarations from the cross. While addressing the seven churches of Asia Minor in Revelation 2 and 3, the Lord is acute at times with exhortation and warnings, but He does not yell to intensify the meaning of His words. If we speak the truth in love (Eph. 4:15), love will need no microphone. There is no cause for those forged into a "one flesh" relationship, who are lifetime companions, to tear down one another through uncontrolled speech for it will only damage the intimacy God intended for the marriage relationship. This should be a foundational rule in measuring issues.

When initial feelings of anger are sensed, one should quickly evaluate and measure the issue. When the first feelings of anger are noticed, determine to ponder the following three concerns for these two questions, and resolution will aid in assessing your attitudes and in levying an appropriate initial response.

"Is this worth getting angry over?"

The discretion of a man deferreth his anger; and it is his glory to pass over a transgression (Prov. 19:11).

Also take no heed unto all words that are spoken; lest thou hear thy servant curse thee (Eccl. 7:21).

"Does my anger have a present righteous purpose?"

Be ye angry, and sin not: let not the sun go down upon your wrath. Neither give place to the devil (Eph. 4:26-27).

Determine to speak softly and avoid unnecessary conflict.

A soft answer turneth away wrath (Prov. 15:1).

One of the techniques the author resorts to when two parties become aggressively vocal in marriage counseling is to utter the word "whisper." It would have been agreed upon previously that both parties would not use their vocal cords to express themselves from that point on but that they would whisper to audibly communicate. It is wearisome to attempt to yell while whispering, and invariably, the couple will transition to laughter as it is futile to express anger through a whisper. The tension of the situation will be immediately squelched, and the counseling session can then continue. Determining to speak softly and politely will likely defuse the other party's anger. Adapt the attitude "don't pester and don't fester." If your speech escalates in volume and intensity, you are effectively taunting the other party to do the same, and the overall tension level will soar exponentially to the point where painful repercussions are inevitable.

> Anger is quieted by a gentle word just as fire is
> quenched by water.
> – Jean Pierre Camus

Determine to think positively.

Nearly two millennia ago Epictetus wrote, "It isn't your problems that are bothering you. It is the way you are looking at them." It has been surmised that 90 percent of life is attitude. What is your natural tendency when you are first cognizant of an awkward situation? Is the glass half full of water or half empty? Do you first notice the beautiful rose blossoms or the prickly thorns? Do you gravitate to favorable thinking first and let the facts dictate otherwise? You should because it will be a salvation to your mind and help you to control unnecessary anger. Sometimes we allow our own imagination to manufacture stomach acids needlessly. We need to think positively about situations and of people.

While visiting a remote region of China, I beheld a crippled man sliding upon his buttocks in the center of a street vigorous with activity. The miserable scene is permanently etched in my mind. Beneath his underside was strapped a frumpy piece of cardboard and a shredded canvas bag; both were being used to reduce the sliding friction, or "road wear," of his backside. His gnarled feet and twisted legs jetted out before him, while his gaunt arms protruded backwards to press against the rough payment. He pushed backwards with earnest rapidity, by yet only gained six to eight inches with each toilsome exertion. He seemed but a prominent rock in a gently flowing stream as pedestrians, carts, and buses nonchalantly altered their intended courses, ever so slightly, so as to causally pass on either side of the beggar. He, the scum of society – a worthless beggar, slunk on through an enormous world of uncertainty and danger. He crept on nearly unnoticed but notably in imminent peril of being instantly crushed by some preoccupied driver. When troublesome circumstances intrude upon my day, I recollect the beggar which instantly causes me to think more positively about by own difficulties – it could be much worse you know.

> *But godliness with contentment is great gain. For we brought nothing into this world, and it is certain we can carry nothing out. And having food and raiment let us be therewith content* (1 Tim. 6:6-8).

Praising God for what we have, rather than complaining about what we don't clutch in our hands, will erect a guard of peace about our minds. The believer must learn contentment, appreciating the blessings and provisions of God, instead of harboring bitterness over perceived shortfalls. At this very moment, your wallet contains exactly what God intends for you to have, or you would have more. The Lord is training us to live frugally, to appreciate what we have, and to rely completely upon Him for all our necessities. Remembering that there are others much worse off than you are will help you to control angry feelings of discontentment and appreciate what you have!

> I was angry, for I had no shoes. Then I met a man
> who had no feet.
>
> – Chinese Proverb

When the matter pertains to people problems, the reader is encouraged to adapt the following three-step approach to maintaining a positive attitude and hopefully alleviating unnecessary angry feelings.

1. **Think positive** – Think upon the positive benefits God could accomplish through the existing disagreeable circumstances or the good deeds that the offending individual has done in the past.

2. **Give the *benefit of the doubt*** – If you can't do (1.), give the offending person the benefit of the doubt until you can obtain accurate facts. *"Then shalt thou inquire, and make search, and ask diligently; and, behold, if it be truth, and the thing certain..."* (Deut. 13:14). It doesn't look good, but until I know for sure I resolve not to think negatively about the errant party.

3 **Don't think about the situation** – If you can't do (2.), determine to put the matter out of your mind. Since we need to think on something, replace the difficult matter with something spiritual (a hymn, spiritual song, Scripture, etc.). If you are not part of

the problem or the solution, determine not to get involved. Simply turn to the Lord, and pray.

Summary Points

The following "first-aid" techniques for controlling initial feelings of anger have been suggested:

1. See and seek God in every situation.
2. Stop, drop and pray.
3. Displace angry thoughts with spiritual ones.
4. Measure the issue.
5. Determine to think positively.

Deflate the Balloon – Channeling Energy and Reducing Tension

In this chapter, we will explore favorable avenues for displacing anger energy in a profitable and productive way. Whether appropriate or not, anger physiologically prepares our bodies for action. Instead of focusing anger energy towards some unsuspecting innocent party in a hostile way, our goal is to harness internal energy to either accomplish some good or redirect and release it safely. The following techniques will assist the reader in easing the internal emotional pressure that anger can abruptly build up.

Physical exercise.

Paul wrote to Timothy that *"bodily exercise profiteth little, but godliness is profitable unto all things"* (1 Tim. 4:8). Commenting on this verse, Warren Wiersbe writes:

Certainly we ought to care for our bodies, and exercise is a part of that care. Our bodies are God's temples, to be used for His glory (1 Cor. 6:19-20), and His tools for His service (Rom. 12:1-2). But bodily exercise benefits us only during this life; godly exercise is profitable now and for eternity. Paul did not ask Timothy to choose between the two; I think

God expects us to practice both. A healthy body can be used of God, but we must major on holiness.[1]

In her book *Total Health Choices for a Winning Lifestyle,* Susan Boe suggests some 20 reasons for incorporating regular exercise into your daily schedule. Many of these pertain to maintaining good physical health, but three of the first four reasons offered relate to improving emotional stability: "Reduces stress and tension and helps you handle the 'unexpected.' Improves your mental alertness and concentration. Helps relieve depression."[2] Regular exercise helps us feel better, live healthier, sleep better and think more clearly. In general, we will have a brighter outlook on life and be more socially connective.

How does exercise help in relieving angry feelings? Anger has prepared our bodies for action, so it is best to allow the energy to flow constructively. Clean the house, do yard work, weed the garden (You can pull a lot of weeds when you're mad.), etc.

Converse with a trusted friend.

Do you have a spiritually-minded friend with whom you can confidently share your faults and weaknesses? A faithful friend that loves you enough to tell you when you are wrong or in error in thought or deed. Finding a friend, who loves the Lord even more than you, is a wonderful provision for your holiness. Solomon upholds the benefit of good friends in the book of Proverbs:

A friend loveth at all times... (Prov. 17:17).

Faithful are the wounds of a friend... (Prov. 27:6).

Ointment and perfume rejoice the heart: so doth the sweetness of a man's friend by hearty counsel (Prov. 27:9).

Iron sharpeneth iron; so a man sharpeneth the countenance of his friend (Prov. 27:17).

Spiritually-minded friends assist us in reproving and removing un-Christ-like qualities from our walk with God. Personal conviction by the Holy Spirit will accompany their counsel and exhortation if it upholds the righteousness of God, that is if one is in fellowship with God. *"If I regard iniquity in my heart, the Lord will not hear me"* (Ps. 66:18).

If your anger has brought on strong anxiety, consulting a trusted counselor may help in thwarting undue fear or the situation being perceived too severely. Sometimes just hearing a calm soothing voice dispels our apprehension over the conjured adversity. A word of caution is here mentioned: be careful not to be too burdensome. Contacting the same person repeatedly will affect their emotional stability – don't pull your friend down into your pit of misery. Don't use them as a stepping stone just so you may see the light of day. Paul provides instruction concerning our responsibility to assist fellow believers in distress:

Brethren, if a man be overtaken in a fault, ye which are spiritual, restore such an one in the spirit of meekness; considering thyself, lest thou also be tempted. <u>Bear ye one another's burdens</u>, and so fulfil the law of Christ. For if a man think himself to be something, when he is nothing, he deceiveth himself. But let every man prove his own work, and then shall he have rejoicing in himself alone, and not in another. <u>For every man shall bear his own burden</u> (Gal. 6:1-5).

At first glance, it seems as if Paul is contradicting himself concerning "bearing burdens." Though the same Greek root word is translated "bear" in verses 2 and 5, a different Greek word is used for "burden" in each verse. In verse 2, Paul exhorts us to bear up one another's *baros,* by implication a "crushing load." However, in verse 5, the instruction is for each believer to bear his or her own *phortion,* speaking of a "mild burden." In Matthew 11:30, the Lord Jesus applied *phortion* to convey a light burden. It is closely identified with the daily weight of the soldier's backpack. There are certain responsibilities and burdens each believer must alone bear with God's help as part of our being a disciple of Christ and our training as soldiers of the cross. There are, however, other times when unforeseen crushing loads wreak havoc upon God's people. At such times, fellow believers are to rally around the despairing comrade, assist them with the load, help them to bear it up, and help them to see Jesus again. Let us not forget that the same One who assigns the crushing loads and daily burdens also *"daily loadeth us with benefits"* (Ps. 68:19).

> I was angry with my friend.
> I told my wrath, my wrath did end.
> I was angry with my foe.
> I told it not, my wrath did grow.
>
> – William Blake

Talk with yourself.
No, we are not suggesting developing a schizophrenic personality or even talking to one's self. Having a dialogue <u>with yourself</u> aloud will often trivialize matters as you listen to yourself speak. It helps to move our thinking from the realm of

imagination into the domain of reality. It also allows some cooling down time to alleviate "flying off the handle" prematurely. Nehemiah put this principle into practice: *"And I was very angry when I heard their cry and these words. Then I con-sulted with myself, and I rebuked the nobles, and the rulers, and said unto them, Ye exact usury, every one of his brother, and I set a great assembly against them"* (Neh. 5:6-7).

Genesis 18:17 should be an encouragement to all of us who occasionally talk with ourselves for God talked with Himself in an audible voice for Abraham's benefit. Though God does not need to reason out uncertain feelings, the incident does show the benefit of audibly talking with one's self.

Laugh

Arnold Glasgow highlighted the benefits of laughter in soothing the human spirit, "Laughter is a tranquilizer with no side effects," while Chuck Swindoll noted that, "Laughter is the most beautiful and beneficial therapy God ever granted humanity." He added, "Laugh out loud. That helps flush out the nervous system."[3] It is true; laughter is "life's shock absorber" and indicates trust in God while in adversity. It is akin to rejoicing, and we are to *"rejoice evermore"* in the Lord (1 Thes. 5:16).

Therefore, pick out a good book, comic strip, etc. that will make you laugh when you need help laughing. I enjoy Ray Comfort's compilation of amusing stories in *Comfort the Feeble Minded*. A good hearty laugh immediately eases internal stress and lessens the weight of life's hardships.

Weep

Oswald Chambers once said, "Laughter and weeping are the two intensest forms of human emotion, and these profound wells of human emotion are to be consecrated to God."[4] *"The sacrifices of God are a broken spirit: a broken and a contrite heart, O God, Thou wilt not despise"* (Ps. 51:17). In the physical realm, when things become broken, value is lost, but in the spiritual realm, God puts a premium on broken things, especially when what is broken is the hearts of His children. If a baseball crashes through the front picture window, I wouldn't gather up the pieces and put them out to be sold at the next garage sale – the window has lost its value; it is unusable. Yet, through brokenness, a believer becomes an *available* vessel of honor for God's good pleasure.

On the eve of confronting Esau, Jacob isolated himself from his family in order to fret over his dilemma. This was a critical point in Jacob's life for he was completely alone with God. To be secluded with God is the only true agency of realizing our frail devices and, more importantly, our depraved hearts. The Lord, incognito, visited Jacob. It is worthy to note that the Lord began the wrestling match with Jacob for Scripture states *"there wrestled a man with him (Jacob)"* (Gen. 32:24), but verse 25 also states, *"he (Jacob) wrestled with Him (the Lord)."* Both the Lord and Jacob desired something from the other. Jacob, nearly 100 years old, wanted a blessing from the Ancient of Days. The Lord wanted Jacob broken and yielded before Him. If the Lord has ever wrestled with the reader, it is for the same purpose – to obtain "brokenness."

The Psalmist proclaims two wonderful promises for those who weep pure tears before the Lord. First, our tears are recorded in God's record book in heaven – poetically, each of them is numbered and collected in a bottle (Ps. 56:8). Secondly, *"They that sow in tears shall reap in joy"* (Ps. 126:5). It is a promise of God that His joy will abundantly fill any void made by tears. Chuck Swindoll put it this way, "a teardrop on earth summons the King of heaven."[5] Women often obtain the benefit from "a good cry" more so than men do – perhaps we men could learn something here. "It is such a secret place, the land of tears" noted Antoine De Saint-Exupery.[6] Crying is a wonderful emotional release, and if the tears are consecrated unto God, He promises to enrich the sorrowful soul with His soothing peace.

Do enjoyable activities.

We are creatures of habit, so it is easy for us to be ensnared in the bondage of daily routines. Busy-ness is one of the greatest enemies of the Church for it means that we have no time to live for God or to enjoy the abundant life Christ has blessed us with. *"I am come that they might have life, and that they might have it more abundantly"* (Jn. 10:10). This life is not to be wasted upon worldliness or selfish ambition but to be lived for Christ. Since we have life in Him, should we not be enjoying our new life? Get out for walks, and enjoy creation. Pray as you stroll, or hum a song as you go. Perhaps meditate on a Scripture you read in your morning quiet time. Attach some memory verses to a clipboard for review while you exercise your body. Plan a family outing; it will offer your mind a break from thinking about life's obstacles. My wife Brenda and I enjoy frequent late afternoon walks together because it is a time to nurture our marriage and to enjoy uninterrupted companionship with each other.

Incorporate into your stressful day a few moments of singing or listening to soothing music. Music is powerful; it can settle the soul (as when David played for King Saul), or it can afflict the soul (as with David and Jeremiah, see Ps. 69:12 and Lam. 3:14, respectively). Music can be employed in pagan worship (Dan. 3:4-6) or to worship God (Ps. 150). If one is full of Christ, acceptable music reflecting humility on our part and adoration towards God will be enjoyed by all God's people (see Rev. 5:9, 14:2-3, 15:2-4). The Lord Jesus, who had a heart that swelled with love for His Father, sang hymns of praise unto His God (Mk. 14:26). Beware of heavy back-beats, strong percussion, off chords or New Age chants. Music is a form of expression, and it is quite possible that tones and rhythms that reek with rebellion will undermine godly words. Music of this nature does not soothe the mind but serves to agitate the flesh and harass one's spirit. Thus, your selection of music is key if you seek for it to calm your nerves.

Summary Points

It is advantageous to emotionally depressurize our inner being. Accomplishing this requires the energy derived from strong emotions to be constantly channeled safely away from individuals, provided righteous indignation is not called for. We need to engage in activities that will reduce tension and exhaust stored up energy before it is regrettably discharged upon some unsuspecting soul. The following activities have been suggested.

1. Routine physical exercise to redirect anger energy constructively.
2. Conversing with a trusted and spiritually-minded friend.
3. Talking with yourself to trivialize the matter.
4. Laughing to release stress.
5. Weeping to reduce emotional tension.
6. Doing enjoyable activities to redirect your thoughts.

Don't Inflate the Balloon –
Resolving Internal Conditions

Anger-motivated behavior must be recognized and repented of before the bent can be transformed. This means getting real with God, no faking, no polite fiction, no excuses, and no delays. Before an individual can come "clean" from a drug addition, he or she must admit that he or she has a problem. Do you have an anger problem? If the answer to this question is yes, and if you have not already done so, fall to your knees right now, tell the Lord all about it, and ask Him to help you to understand the core internal conditions that cause you to be an angry person.

Once the internal conditions within your inner man are identified and understood, resolution of each condition must be sought. Terminating internal conditions minimizes the opportunities for repressurizing the inner man after first-aid has brought temporary anger relief. Ideally, there should be no internal pressure within the balloon; thus, no opportunity to pop it (i.e. vent unclean anger).

What is the common denominator among all of our internal conditions? Pride, in one form or another. Pride is self-focusing, either in condescending attitudes that promote our own stateliness, pity parties that seek to impose guilt upon others, or the desire to be the center of attention. Love of display is for prostitutes and court jesters, not God's children. The bottom line, pride must be deflated. *"Only by pride cometh contention"* (Prov. 13:10). The psalmist accurately describes those choosing to continue in wickedness: *"pride compasseth them about like a chain; violence covereth them like a garment"* (Ps. 73:6). Before one can affect positive behavioral change one must call sin – sin. If all contention is motivated by pride, we must then conclude that anger-motivated sin is pride-based. Pride comes from being high on self. It might be self-wants, self-exaltation, self-pity or selfishness, but self-focus is the common ill.

No wonder God hates pride (Prov. 6:16-17) because pride neglects the interests of others. God is love (1 Jn. 4:8), and biblical love initiates by giving – it sacrifices self. *"For <u>God so loved</u> the world, that <u>He gave His</u> only begotten Son, that whosoever believeth in Him should not perish, but have everlasting life"* (Jn. 3:16). God and His love are perfect – He has no internal conditions. His anger always responds righteously to the foreknown external conditions that our rebel race imposes upon Him. If our love were devoid of pride, our anger would always serve God and others because we would have no rage or resentment problems to hinder selflessness.

Step 1: Face Your Anger

Pertaining to our spiritual walk, pride is a boundless snare to our feet. The first step to recovery is to admit that we have an anger problem and to assume full responsibility for our actions which means yielding and accepting the Scriptural boundaries of authority and conduct God has ordered for our lives. Secondly, it means apologizing to those towards whom we have expressed unclean anger. Admitting that we have erred is a sign of personal strength and demonstrates practical contentment with who we are in Christ. Genuinely humbling ourselves practically verifies our comprehension of being fully accepted by God in the Beloved (Eph. 1:6) and our abandonment of all self-promoting systems of "doings" to impress God. Personal pride is no longer the grout holding our old self-concocted faith system together. Paul proclaimed, *"For I determined not to know any thing among you, save Jesus Christ, and Him crucified"* (1 Cor. 2:2), and *"He that glorieth, let him glory in the Lord"* (1 Cor. 1:31). Glorying in Christ alone means the believer will attend to his or her character and commit his or her reputation to the Lord's care.

Thirdly, anger recovery will seek restoration. If your actions have injured another or caused them loss, you should promptly offer restitution and, as much as possible, restore what was lost or damaged to original conditions (Mt. 5:23-26). In the Levitical system, the sin offering was commanded for the *offense of sin*, but the trespass offering was required for the *damages of sin*. Both were non-sweet savor offerings because God took no pleasure in them. He demanded both offerings from those committing sins of ignorance (There were no personal offerings for willful sin!). Through these two offerings, God was practically teaching His children to apologize and make restitution for wrongdoing.

Proverbs 20:5 reads, *"Counsel in the heart of man is like deep water, but a man of understanding will draw it out."* Biblical counseling uses the illumination of God's Word to explore the dark recesses of man's depraved heart then draws out into the light what is not of God and what must, consequently, be eradicated. After the sword of truth wields evil thinking a mortal blow, the counselor then implants what is living and true into the heart-void just created. Accountability is then applied to ensure that what is Christ-like holds fast and that evil does not creep back in.

The following questions and tools provide the angry person with an honest heart examination, an opportunity to see your heart condition as the Great Physician does. He already knows what the ailment is, and He longs for you to know about it, too.

I. Why can't I say "I'm sorry"?

One of the main reasons we fail to admit our mistakes and failures to others is that we feel vulnerable and unprotected from the consequences of such information being made public. Ultimately, fear-based pride (a self-preserving focus to maintain status) hinders us from admitting our errors.

1. Am I inclined to deny rendering mistakes in judgment?

2. Do I readily admit my imperfections to others?

3. Do I practice "no-fault" problem resolution, or am I more intent on affixing blame to the guilty?

4. Do I have a problem relating to those in authority or, in general, with someone telling me what to do?

5. Do I naturally focus on the mistakes of others before acknowledging my own failures?

6. What means do I use to evade accountability or to keep my weaknesses from being exposed?

7. When confronted for a known personal mistake, do I tend to defend my actions or to blame others for my blunder?

8. Do I feel rejected or abandoned by others when I do admit my failures?

9. Am I more focused on the opinions of others than on pleasing the Lord?

II. Admitting wrongdoing.
1. When I do apologize, do I affirm love to the person I have offended?

2. Does my apology seek to control or manipulate the other party, or is it heartfelt and remorseful?

3. When apologizing, do I tend to criticize or blame others for my errors rather than accepting full responsibility for my actions?

4. Do my apologies include "if" statements, or do I concisely admit my offense and ask for forgiveness?

5. Are my apologies to others coldly mechanical or framed in sincerity?

6. Do I tend to "beat around the bush" or be specific about my true feelings?

7. How might I make restitution for wronging others to prove that I am legitimately sorry for my poor conduct?

Step 2: Evaluate Your Anger

After confession and restitution, the next step of healing is to seek God's wisdom and help, which may be partly found through the counsel of other "godly" believers who both know and love you.

I. Why am I angry?

"Why did I get so upset over that?" What was the root cause of my anger? Many techniques are available that may be used to discover the answer to this question. The reader may find the following methods helpful in identifying resident internal conditions (the root cause of your anger):

1. Keep an anger notebook.

In my opinion, this technique has proven to be the most effective in exploring core anger causes. Carry a small notebook with you wherever you go. When you have angry thoughts, write down the event (date, time, place, setting, etc.), why you felt angry, how you handled your anger, how others responded to you, and lastly, how you felt about the way you handled your anger. You must do this immediately after each event, or you will forget the details, and the exercise will lose value. Sit down regularly (on a weekly basis is recommended at first) with a Christian counselor to help you to decipher the information, to identify trends and to determine if you might have responded in a more appropriate manner. Be sure to offer thanks to the Lord for the victories and to pray over the mistakes specifically.

2. Memory recollection.

Unresolved anger from previous events may be injected into present situations or at individuals who don't deserve our unclean anger responses. I have discovered that a high percentage of those struggling with anger were abused as children (sexually, physically, verbally, etc.). Frequently, mistreated and demeaned children later enter into adulthood with low self-worth. These internal conditions are usually deep-seated, as many years have usually passed. Often much or most of the details about the situation are lost, but the pain is remembered. This traps some individuals in the ironic dilemma of "I know I am angry, but I don't quite remember why?" The internal condition becomes more difficult to resolve if our imaginations fill in missing details. Eventually, we have a painful altered reality into which truth must find its way for healing to occur. Try asking yourself the following questions to ensure that you are not reflecting unresolved anger upon others who don't deserve it:

(1) Did I perceive that the event that made me angry had happened to me before? If so, when?

(2) Did I unknowingly associate the person who angered me with someone else who has previously hurt me (perhaps his or her mannerism, appearance, smell, voice, a smirk, etc.)?

(3) Did the circumstances remind me of a past experience (perhaps childhood related) that was similar?

(4) Did I feel that I was being forced into a mold or to do something in the same way or through the same means that someone else had previously tried?

(5) Do I remember all the facts concerning this incident accurately? Could there be missing details?

(6) Did I receive from my parent(s) more criticism than positive communication about my behavior? Did I feel as if I could never meet their expectations which then made me feel inadequate in their eyes?

(7) Even though I am an adult, am I still driven to try to please my parents and I am often anxious about what they may think of my lifestyle, marriage partner, parenting skills, family life and profession?

Note: We should respect our parents throughout life, but the focus here is on feeling vulnerable to perceived or expressed parental attitudes or feeling inferior in the presence of a long-standing controlling parental spirit.

3. **Review unmet needs.**
Sometimes our anger is associated with needs that we feel are deserved but which remain unmet. Evaluate your "need" anticipation by answering the following questions:

(1) What are my legitimate needs in life (e.g. time alone, money, affections, etc.)?

(2) What are some recent examples of when I concluded that these needs were not met?

(3) How have these unmet needs affected my emotional disposition?

(4) How should I rightly respond to those associated with not satisfying my legitimate needs?

(5) What would be warning signs to me that I am too self-focused in having my needs met?

Frankly speaking, the reader will generally find that selfishness is the root cause of this type of anger. Perhaps after answering these questions, you will prove this point to yourself also. It is a natural lust of our fallen flesh to have our own way, *"But godliness with contentment is great gain"* (1 Tim. 6:6).

II. What was my motive for being angry?

What was the real purpose of my anger? Often hidden base motives lay dormant in our minds until the opportunity avails itself for these self-seeking agendas to rear up center stage in our thinking. Evaluate your true motives for becoming angry.

1. Was my expressed anger intended for the glorification of God?

2. Was my expressed anger for the purpose of serving others?

3. Was my anger selfish? Did my anger produce an emotional rush, seize the attention of others, make me feel powerful, or result in someone else suffering unrighteously or being distressed?

4. Did I feel guilty after expressing my anger?

5. If applicable, why did I hold on to my anger so long? Was I afraid of anything?

6. If so, was the guilt because of poor behavior on my part or because I felt sorry for the one I expressed my anger to?

   Note: True love abounds in knowledge (Phil. 1:9) – it seeks what is best for others. Thus, love, not the pity we feel for those suffering the consequences of self-imposed sin, must motivate our actions. We should not be motivated to action unless the overall good of the individual is served. If motivated by pity, not by love, we may undermine God's dealings with an individual in sin. God chastens those He loves in order to bring the erring child of God back into fellowship with Himself (Heb. 12:6).

7. Am I holding a grudge against the person I was angered by? If so, why?

8. Did I get angry with another person because I felt he or she devalued me in some facet of my life? In this area of my life, do I place more value on what they think or on what God thinks about it?

9. Do I get angry when my preferences in life are not adhered to? What makes me so intolerant of the opinions or mannerisms of others in this area of preference?

Why do I feel my way is the only right way to do something?

10. Do I get angry with others who do not hold my convictions on proper conduct? Anger often demonstrates insecurity in what one truly believes, so why am I getting angry when others do not conform to my standard of right and wrong? Do I let my anger expressions console my fears of possibly being wrong?

III. How should I have responded?
"Hindsight is 20-20." Knowing the aftermath of our actions while angry enables us to evaluate our effectiveness in properly using anger to accomplish good. Evaluating history affords us the opportunity to conclude whether our behavior is being controlled by external events or personal choices. Generally speaking, there are only two right responses for our anger: **resolution** (letting the offense go and releasing the anger associated with the offense) or **indignation** (let my anger promote godly action).

1. Did my behavior while angry exhibit the fruit of the Spirit (Gal. 5:22-23)?

2. Did my behavior while angry transgress God's commandments (Jn. 14:15)?

3. Did my behavior stumble a weaker brother (1 Cor. 8:9-12)?

4. Did my behavior compromise my testimony as an ambassador of Christ (1 Cor. 9:12, 10:33)?

5. Was my behavior wise or foolish (Rom. 16:19)?

6. Did my behavior promote peace and healthy spiritual growth in others (Rom. 14:19)?

7. Did my behavior glorify God (1 Cor. 10:31)?

8. Did I allow my imagination to fill in details that were not actual reality? If so, how can I better anchor my mind in truth the next time I am challenged in the same way?

9. What could I have done differently to better achieve the righteousness of God in the situation?

Step 3: Release Unclean Anger and Work Clean Anger

"That's the straw that broke the camel's back." Often the circumstance that caused the mushroom cloud of rage was not the real issue at all. If unresolved anger accumulates, the pressure within our inner man increases. Eventually, the slightest external condition will result in an outburst of rage, often against an innocent bystander.

I. Confronting those who make us angry.

If we determine that we are angry for a righteous purpose, it is appropriate for us to lovingly confront those who have angered us. We must take responsibility for our anger to properly allow it to serve God and others; otherwise, the strong feelings will accumulate. The following Scriptures provide both the motive for confronting others and insights in how to rightly challenge people.

Open rebuke is better than secret love (Prov. 27:5).

He that rebuketh a man afterwards shall find more favour than he that flattereth with the tongue (Prov. 28:23).

Moreover if thy brother shall trespass against thee, go and tell him his fault between thee and him alone: if he shall hear thee, thou hast gained thy brother. But if he will not hear thee, then take with thee one or two more, that in the mouth of two or three witnesses every word may be established. And if he shall neglect to hear them, tell it unto the church: but if he neglect to hear the church, let him be unto thee as an heathen man and a publican (Mt. 18:15-17).

A ruckus between two sisters in the church of Philippi was adversely affecting the unity of the whole assembly. Paul skillfully confronted Euodia and Syntyche in a three-step approach (Phil. 4:1-3). First, he affirmed his love for them, then exhorted them to know the mind of Christ (and, thus, to aspire to godly conduct), and finally acknowledged their good works in the name of Christ. He sandwiched the negative between the two positive statements. Often the last thing said in a conversation is what people remember best.

II. Release offenses immediately.

"And be ye kind one to another, tenderhearted, forgiving one another, even as God for Christ's sake hath forgiven you" (Eph. 4:32). If the believer has been wronged and no present righteous purpose can be served by his or her anger, the believer must then release the offense unto the Lord's care and wait until action can be ensued. The adverse situation can then be quickly ushered from the foreground to the background of our thinking until God's time allows resolution. The chapters entitled *Seeking Forgiveness* and *Receiving Forgiveness* ad-

dress in detail the matters of releasing offenses, obtaining forgiveness and defeating bitterness.

III. Extend forgiveness.

When an offending individual repents and confesses their sin to you, you must forgive them for the Lord commands it.

> *Take heed to yourselves: If thy brother trespass against thee, rebuke him; and if he repent, forgive him. And if he trespass against thee seven times in a day, and seven times in a day turn again to thee, saying, I repent; thou shalt forgive him* (Lk. 17:3-4).

After forgiveness is conveyed, the matter should be forgotten from the standpoint that the offense has been resolved. *"Love keeps no record of wrongs"* (1 Cor. 13:5 NIV). With this said, forgiveness is not blind; it remembers the weakness in order to avoid undue injury in the future until trust is gained through repeated right-doing by the offending party. Forgiveness relates to the specific offense but wisely recalls the behavior until it has been mastered. Recalling is for the purpose of assisting the offending parties in personal growth, not for reminding them of past failures that have already been forgiven.

Don't permit angry feelings to accumulate. Assume responsibility for your behavior. Either "let anger go" or "turn to godly action." If your anger does not have a present righteous purpose, you must release it. Cain quickly learned that murder was an accessible door in his heart that anger effortlessly opened.

Summary Points

1. Unclean anger finds its root in pride (an unscriptural self-focus).

2. Facing our anger requires us to take full responsibility for it. Admitting that we have a problem, confessing our sin to those we have offended, and seeking restitution demonstrates good anger stewardship.

3. Evaluating our anger requires us to sincerely analyze both our motives for being angry and the outcome of our behavior. Did my anger serve God, others, or myself?

4. Releasing unclean anger and working clean anger will require us to immediately render to God's care all offenses which cannot be resolved righteously and promptly. We must take personal responsibility to resolve our angry feelings as they occur (That is, after we have gained proper emotional composure.) To do this will require us to confront others in a loving way, to offer forgiveness when sin is confessed, and to assist them in improving their deficient behavior.

Don't Jab the Balloon –
Minimizing External Conditions

Twenty years of married life have shown my wife and I just how prone our flesh is to envy and strife. I recall two particular events in those early days of marital discovery that perfectly affirm the words Jeremiah spoke so long ago, *"The heart is deceitful above all things, and desperately wicked; who can know it?"* (Jer. 17:9). As newlyweds, we occasionally played a two-handed game of Rook. Yet, in the course of time, it became apparent that one of us was enjoying the game less and less – in fact one of us never won. One evening, in utter frustration, the cards were thrown across the table, and a bruised ego declared, "I never want to play this game again!" And we didn't – for nearly ten years in fact. Now, we play the same game purely for recreation, and no discord is realized. What changed? It is the same game, but we are different people. More specifically, we are more like Christ in our attitudes than we were twenty years ago. Practical sanctification is a life-long pursuit and work of God. Praise God that He loves us too much to permit us to remain as we are!

The second event centers around the game of tennis. My wife taught me how to play, and at least initially, we both enjoyed playing tennis together, but one of us rarely won. Then, the day came in which one of us assaulted a steel pylon with their tennis racket. The law of conservation of energy held firm, and the tennis racket was promptly reshaped into something that better resembled the letter "C" on a stick. That ended all tennis activities for some time, but now we again enjoy the game with no competitive spirit at all – in fact, we don't care to even keep score. I kept that contorted tennis racket for a number of years as a testimony of what my own flesh is capable of doing. Yes, it was I.

Refrain from anger and turn from wrath; do not fret--it leads only to evil (Ps. 37:8 NIV).

The order of verbs within this verse serves a practical warning if not heeded: "refrain," "turn," "fret," and "leads." One must both cease and turn from anger to elude self-inflicted emotional pain and to avoid committing sin. A garage that specialized in automotive brake repair proudly advertised "If you can't stop – don't start" – this is good advice for the Christian, too. Examine yourself. If you determine an area of moral weakness or a propensity of your flesh to sin, don't flirt with disaster. Forethought and resolve are effective in precluding sin. A recovering drunk should not venture near the saloon, nor should the repentant thief tarry too long at the open cash register drawer. *"But put ye on the Lord Jesus Christ, and make not provision for the flesh, to fulfil the lusts thereof"* (Rom. 13:14). No provision means, **no provision** – avoid solicitations to be angry when possible. Unrighteous anger is a work of the flesh (Gal. 5:20).

What about individuals who just seem to abruptly get under your skin and raise your dander? Avoid them, but don't shun them. Don't engage in close association with them, but don't evade them either. If you notice such a person while grocery shopping, don't deliberately crouch behind a stack of toilet paper to avoid being seen. Be polite and cordial, but refrain from intimate discourse. If a forced discussion occurs, keep it on a "surface level" – burrowing into details will only provide opportunity for jabs, sarcasm and an altercation. By no means could this be considered the long-term solution, but it does afford you an opportunity to acquire emotional composure until a beneficial encounter can be anticipated.

The majority of my adolescent years were spent laboring on a cattle ranch in Kansas. When I was 12, my boss instructed me on how to work closely with cattle and survive, "keep right up next to 'em or keep clear away, that mid-area is where you will get the stuffing kicked out of you." I didn't regard the warning at first, but after being knocked to the ground the second time, I thoroughly understood the advice and heeded it. Consequently, I was never bruised again. To engage a rude person in conversation is much like managing a disagreeable cow; you either stay right next to them to reduce hostile protocol, or you remain at a safe distance to avoid the kick altogether. To simply put it, no jab means no potential for anger! Why needlessly put yourself in harm's way when you are already aware of your weakness and the emotional threat.

Lastly, the best means of limiting irritating circumstances that arouse anger is to stay nigh to the Lord. The closer we draw to Christ, the less sensitive we will be about non-essential matters. We will also be less desirous of self-promotion. *"He must increase, but I must decrease"* (Jn. 3:30). As the balloon skin thickens, the pinpricks pose less of a threat. Might we all have thicker skin. Paul wrote, *"I obtained mercy, that in me first Jesus Christ might show all longsuffering, as a pattern to those who are going to believe on Him for everlasting life"* (1 Tim. 1:16 NKJV). Not only do we experience His peace through close fellowship, but we learn His mind and are better equipped spiritually to measure our weaknesses and discern foolishness.

The matter of knowing right and wrong behavior is dependent upon knowing the commandments of Scripture. Discernment of what is wise and what is foolish behavior is dependent upon knowing God's commandments, warnings, principles, promises, and the "lessons learned" from personal narratives in Scripture, as well as being sensitive to the Holy Spirit's leading. Interestingly, the Lord spoke more often of being wise and not foolish than of what was right and wrong conduct (although the latter would certainly be included in what is wise and foolish behavior). The motive for doing what is right and wise is found in loving Christ (Jn. 14:15). *"Ye that love the Lord, hate evil"* (Ps. 97:10). If the child of God loves the Savior, he or she will submit to divine commands and consent to spiritual wisdom. Don't call Him Lord if you're not going to do what He says (Lk. 6:46).

Summary Points

1. Avoid trouble – walk around the situations that you know will tend to prompt ill temper.
2. Don't closely associate with individuals who easily arouse your dander.
3. Maintaining close fellowship with Christ will minimize situations that provoke poor behavior and offer spiritual wisdom to handle the ones that still do.

Seeking Forgiveness

Bitterness is truly a self-imposed affliction that literally "presses down on the heart." It can plague the church and affect every relationship the bitter individual has, including open fellowship with the Lord, but it can be defeated by forgiveness. If we realize that others will naturally hurt us, we should also recognize that developing a forgiving heart is a necessary part of interacting with each other. Certainly, God's children, our friends, and even the unsaved are not our enemies; therefore, we must learn to forgive them, or we will impose an adversarial disposition on the relationship.

Watchman Nee understood this matter: "Aside from Satan, the Lord has no enemies, only potential friends," and "If we have died and indeed we have in Christ it should be impossible to be offended." Early in his Christian walk, Nee realized his evangelistic ministry had been stifled because he had offended others and not asked for their forgiveness. He then created a list of those he had potentially offended and apologized to each one. Immediately, he witnessed dozens of souls being won to Christ.[1] Bitterness can stifle the Spirit of God from working in our lives.

Two Greek words in the New Testament are primarily translated "forgive." *Aphiemi* (af-ee'-ay-mee) is the most common and may also be translated "leave," "suffer," "give," "sent away," "yield up," or "put away." *Aphiemi* is associated with the act of forgiving 48 times in the New Testament, but oddly, it is only employed four times in all of the epistles in speaking of forgiveness. We must realize that it is humanly possible to forgive and not forget, and to forget and not forgive; therefore, forgetting is not forgiving. This aspect of forgiving declares that the wrong has been put away and will not be remembered any more. *Aphiemi* primarily means "to send forth" or "to send away" (*apo*, "from," *hiemi*, "to send") or by implication "to forgive." It views God's willful action of sending away the remembrance of our sin as illustrated in Psalm 103:12: *"As far as the east is from the west, so far hath He removed our transgressions from us,"* or in Hebrews 10:17, *"Their sins and iniquities will I remember no more."*

The second Greek word used to speak of forgiveness in the New Testament is *charizomai* (khar-id'-zom-ahee) which means "to bestow a favor unconditionally or to freely give or release." Interestingly, 14 of the 24 times *charizomai* is found in the New Testament, it is translated as some variation of "forgive." Even more fascinating is that 12 of these 14 occurrences are located in the Epistles. The only two occurrences of *charizomai* in the Gospel accounts are found together in one parable (Luke 7). Paul explained the motive for "releasing" the desire for vengeance and retribution:

> *Forbearing one another, and forgiving one another, if any man have a quarrel against any:* ***even as Christ forgave you, so also do ye"*** (Col. 3:13).

> *And be ye kind one to another, tenderhearted, forgiving one another,* ***even as God for Christ's sake hath forgiven you"*** (Eph. 4:32).

How do these two different words relate to the activity of forgiving each other? The mechanics of forgiveness (how to send away offenses) seems to be associated with the word *aphiemi*, while *charizomai* addresses the motive for releasing the offender with an unconditional attitude. The "how to's" include going privately to a brother who has offended you (Mt. 18:15), or to a brother who has been offended by you (Mt. 5:23-24) to seek resolution. If there is acknowledgement of the sin, a declaration of forgiveness should then follow the offending party's confession and repentance. We must be willing to repeatedly declare forgiveness to those who repent of the offense (Mt. 18:21-22). General Oglethorpe said to John Wesley, "I never forgive!," to which Wesley replied, "Then, sir, I hope you never sin."[2] The fact is that we do sin and that we do need the forgiveness of others and of the Lord Jesus. Let us not withhold from others what we have freely received.

Why are the mechanics of forgiveness spoken of in the Gospel accounts, but the motive to forgive found in the Epistles? Prior to Calvary, the motive to forgive (Christ's suffering for our sin that we might be forgiven) was not evident, which is why *aphiemi* is predominantly applied in the Gospels and *charizomai* is found in the Epistles. *Aphiemi* speaks of the process and mindset of forgiveness, while *charizomai* implores us "to freely release" in light of what we have been forgiven.

So how does scriptural forgiveness work? As soon as the believer has been offended, he or she must "freely release" all self-right to exact vengeance and to get even. Whatever the matter, it is less painful and distasteful than the Lord Jesus bearing our sin under divine judgment; therefore, you should deliver the matter to the Lord to resolve. *"Dearly beloved, avenge not yourselves, but rather give place unto wrath: for it is written, Vengeance is Mine; I will repay, saith the Lord"*

(Rom. 12:19). Then, when you have control of your emotions, the guilty party should be confronted. If he repents, you have won a brother, and you should verbally declare forgiveness to him (2 Cor. 2:7-8). If he does not repent, you should not seize the situation back from the Lord, for you have released it to Him as a sweet smelling sacrifice (1 Pet. 2:19-20). Releasing means it will not affect the "foreground" of your daily affairs but will remain in the "background" of your thinking so that when the offending party does repent you are quite willing and ready to declare forgiveness. It is unbiblical to declare forgiveness to someone without them first acknowledging that their behavior is wrong. To declare forgiveness to an offending party prior to them admitting their sin is an affront to God's righteousness and serves only to promote a continuance of sin.

> The sandal-tree perfumes when riven the ax that laid it low;
> Let man, who hopes to be forgiven, forgive and bless his foe.

> – Sadi

Receiving Forgiveness

For those suffering from anger-motivated behavior, it is important to pause and count the cost of your past rage and resentment. Take a few moments, and jot down all the consequences of your anger that you can recall. Contemplate past damaged relationships, severed friendships, emotionally scarred children, broken and damaged property, lost employment, etc. How did your past behavior bring reproach upon the name of Christ? If you have not done so, repent of these past sins, and ask God for His forgiveness and healing. Since believers have a standing of righteousness in Christ after conversion, the purpose of confessing sin is to be brought back into fellowship with God. Our relationship depends upon spiritual birth into God's family, but our communion with Him depends upon our behavior.

> *If we say that we have no sin, we deceive ourselves, and the truth is not in us. If we confess our sins, He is faithful and just to forgive us our sins, and to cleanse us from all unrighteousness. If we say that we have not sinned, we make Him a liar, and His Word is not in us* (1 Jn. 1:8-10).

The believer must endeavor to keep "short accounts" with the Lord Jesus. The moment wrong thoughts enter our minds or inappropriate actions are committed, we should quickly confess the sin and turn from the wrong behavior. Through the finished work of Christ, God is quite capable of righteously dealing with man's sin. Listen to what the Old Testament writers declare about God's long-suffering character concerning the forgiveness of our sin.

Come now, and let us reason together, saith the Lord: though your sins be as scarlet, they shall be as white as snow; though they be red like crimson, they shall be as wool (Isa. 1:18).

As far as the east is from the west, so far hath He removed our transgressions from us (Ps. 103:12).

Who is a God like unto Thee, that pardoneth iniquity, and passeth by the transgression of the remnant of His heritage? He retaineth not His anger forever, because He delighteth in mercy. He will turn again, He will have compassion upon us; He will subdue our iniquities; and thou wilt cast all their sins into the depths of the sea (Micah 7:18-19).

Through the propitiation of Christ's sacrifice, the above Scripture poetically describes His just dealings with man's sin: He bleaches sin to remove its stain, plunges it beneath the depths of the sea to behold it no more, and completely removes sin's essence from any map of earthly recognition. North and South may meet, but East and West never do. He eternally removes sin from our account and from His own remembrance. How a sovereign omniscient God chooses not to remember confessed sin is a miracle beyond human comprehension. Though God chooses not to remember, the believer will find it helpful to recollect what mire he or she has been saved from through the blood of Christ. One need not feel guilt over what has been forgiven, but remembering the terrible cost of your rage and resentment will provide an extra incentive not to return to what has grieved God, hurt others and offered you nothing but misery and pain.

A zealous Pharisee named Saul had been guilty of imprisoning and slaughtering men and women for their unwavering faith in Jesus Christ. Saul became the Apostle Paul after his conversion to Christ and, by his own reasoning, reckoned that these pernicious deeds had qualified him to be not only the least of the apostles (1 Cor. 15:9) but, in fact, the least of the saints of God (Eph. 3:8). With this said, Paul knew that his present and future life in Christ was far more important than the legalism he had ignorantly pursued without Christ. Though lacking complete maturity, he explained to the saints at Philippi, *"This one thing I do, forgetting those things which are behind, and reaching forth unto those things which are before, I press toward the mark for the prize of the high calling of God in Christ Jesus"* (Phil. 3:13-14*)*.

Have you murdered anyone lately or blasphemed the name of Jesus Christ? Hopefully not. If God could forgive Paul of his wretched past then use him so mightily to further His kingdom, might He also use those of us who have lapsed in our faith and miserably failed Him altogether? Christian maturity may require years, but it is never a matter of years. It requires time but is not achieved by age; it requires experience, but is not dependent upon life's events. Maturity rightly divides the best from the rest and then presses on toward the prize of God's upward calling in Christ.

Solomon wrote, *"For a just man falleth seven times, and riseth up again: but the wicked shall fall into mischief"* (Prov. 24:16). It is not falling, but failing to rise up again that ensures one of being a failure in life. Groveling and wallowing in self-pity after stumbling, simply put, hinders the Lord from accomplishing the spectacular in our lives, and in this sense, we defy the Lordship of Christ. We are no less guilty than Abraham who presumptuously sought a child of the flesh through Hagar rather than waiting any longer for the child of divine promise. *"They that are in the flesh cannot please God"* (Rom. 8:8). What is not complete reliance on God is of the flesh. True faith is deaf to beckoning lusts of the flesh, *"for whatever is not of faith is sin"* (Rom. 14:23). Human doubt in response to God's inerrant immutable word is offensive to God. Thank the Lord, *"If we believe not, yet He abideth faithful; He cannot deny Himself"* (2 Tim. 2:13). The righteous man gleans maturity from his mistakes and commits to the Lord both his failures and the need for grace to abstain from future foolhardiness. Staying down ensures failure, but rising again in Christ dependence is victory! *"For whatsoever is born of God overcometh the world: and this is the victory that overcometh the world, even our faith"* (1 Jn. 5:4).

So, beloved get on with your life in Christ, confess your failures, repent of your sins, receive His forgiveness and accept His grace for the future. The Lord Jesus did not journey from heaven's glory to a cursed earth only to die for sinners and offer eternal life to humanity. He desires much more than that, for He longs for every believer to taste Him presently and to live out His abundant life now (Jn. 10:10)! God promises to forgive the repentant soul (1 Jn. 1:9), so arise, unshackle your regrets, free your guilt, release your anger and walk afresh in the newness and sweetness of Christ. Be free to serve!

Concluding Devotion

We have explored God's Word for discernment, counsel and encouragement. *"For the word of God is quick, and powerful, and sharper than any two-edged sword, piercing even to the dividing asunder of soul and spirit, and of the joints and marrow, and is a discerner of the thoughts and intents of the heart"* (Heb. 4:12). The Bible is a living textbook that exposes our true heart condition while the Holy Spirit instructs us as to what our heart should be. As we draw our study on anger to a close, may we do so by considering Christ again. For if we learn but not learn of Him, we have failed in our calling and our pursuit of God's peace.

The Bible contains many examples of God's righteous anger and subsequent wrath for an important purpose. *"Who knoweth the power of Thine anger? Even according to Thy fear, so is Thy wrath. So teach us to number our days, that we may apply our hearts unto wisdom"* (Ps 90:11-12). *"The fear of the Lord is the beginning of knowledge: but fools despise wisdom and instruction"* (Prov. 1:7). Sodom and Gomorrah were incinerated, Egypt was plagued, and Korah was swallowed alive into the belly of the earth for our learning. God is not mocked – He will recompense wrath for evil doings. The fear of God leads us to God's peace in Christ.

Perhaps the most notable example of God's righteous wrath over man's sin is seen in the flood of Noah's day (Gen. 6-8).

"God saw that the wickedness of man was great in the earth, and that every imagination of the thoughts of his heart was only evil continually" (Gen. 6:5). In all, only eight souls were saved from God's wrath because they alone had entered the ark that they had built by faith. Their faith was based solely on the Word of God – no signs were given to Noah to believe. He simply took God at His word, and it was accounted to him as righteousness.

The ark itself is a type of Christ. In the broad sense, the ark pictures the safety that Christ offers to all who will enter into His own body, the Church, by faith. Before the ark could be constructed, building materials were needed – gopher trees had to be cut down. The death of these trees pictures the humanity of Christ in that only through His sacrifice could spiritual life for man be secured. Since trees don't have blood, God was careful to apply some to the ark so that we would not miss the "type." The word translated *"pitch"* in Genesis 6:14 is most often translated "atonement" (nearly 75 times in the Old Testament). Prior to Calvary, man's sin could only be atoned for (covered) by the blood of animals through sacrifices. The fact that the ark was pitched from within and without further shadows the future suffering and sacrifice of Christ. From His wounds, redemptive blood would rudely and profusely coat His body then drip and splatter upon the ground. The word usage and the typology of Genesis 6 both convey the visage of a bleeding ark, thus, picturing the suffering Savior at Calvary.

Only one door provided entrance into the ark (Gen. 6:16), and only God could shut it (Gen. 7:16) once all those who entered by faith were within. It would be God who judged the earth for man's wickedness (Gen. 6:7); thus, the very ark that Noah had built would know God's wrath. However, while the ark bore the judgment of Almighty God, all the souls that were in the ark were kept safe from judgment. The Lord Jesus said He was the only door (Jn. 10:9) and the only way (Jn. 14:6), and He bore the judgment of God for man's sin once and for all (Heb. 9:26-28, 10:9-18). The Lord said, *"whosoever liveth and believeth in Me shall never die"* (Jn. 11:26). Our soul's security rests in the hand (Jn. 10:28-29) and the sealing power of God (Eph. 1:13). We never read of water pouring through the door to despair Noah's family or of any family member being lost at sea. When God sealed the door shut, it was securely closed, and when God seals the believer in Christ, he or she is maintained securely within.

Genesis 7:1 contains the first command of God to *"come"* in the Bible. It is the first gospel invitation – come into the ark, and find security and safety from the wrath to come. It is evident by God's communication that He was already in the ark and waiting for Noah to come in; otherwise, He would have commanded Noah to "go into the ark." Once in the ark, what words in Scripture could possibly describe the security of the believer in Christ more clearly than the words *"the Lord shut him in"* (Gen. 7:16). The hand of God closed the only door, thus, sealing Noah's family safely within. The opportunity for salvation had come to a close, and only those choosing to come through the door were saved. The Lord Jesus said, *"I am the door, by Me if any man enter in, he shall be saved"* (Jn. 10:9).

The flood, the parable of Luke 14:15-24, and the admonition of Proverbs 1:24-33 serve as solemn warnings that God's judicial anger will be expressed against all those who reject His gracious invitation to repent and be saved. May we eternally appreciate Calvary, where God's wrath for our sin fell upon an innocent and willing substitute – Christ. *"Seek ye the Lord while He may be found, call ye upon Him while He is near: Let the wicked forsake his way, and the unrighteous man his thoughts: and let him return unto the Lord, and He will have mercy upon him; and to our God, for He will abundantly pardon"* (Isa. 55:6-7).

Indebted and undone, hath none to bring;
Behold Me then: Me for him, life for life
I offer: on Me let Thine anger fall;
Account Me Man; I for his sake will leave
Thy bosom, and this glory next to Thee

Freely put off, and for him lastly die
Well pleased; on Me let Death wreak all his rage.
Under his gloomy power I shall not long
Lie vanquished. Thou hast given Me to possess
Life in Myself for ever; by Thee I live;

Milton's *Paradise Lost* (Book 3)

The Cover

Have you noticed the way in which Paul commences each of his epistles? *"Grace be unto you, and peace, from God our Father, and from the Lord Jesus Christ"* (Phil. 1:2). Sometimes his salutations include *mercy* between *grace* and *peace*, but in each of his letters, *grace* always precedes *peace*. A work of grace needs to be accomplished in our hearts before peace will reside there. God must do a work upon us and within us if we ever want to know His peace – *"the peace of God, which passeth all understanding, shall keep your hearts and minds through Christ Jesus"* (Phil. 4:7).

For this reason, it is necessary for us to understand and evaluate our anger with scriptural illumination and spiritual discernment. Our righteous anger must then be yielded up to God for His use and glory. In some cases, where we are suffering amiss, this process will require us to release our anger. In doing so, we will offer a sweet-smelling sacrifice for suffering wrongly. Man cannot beguile time, and, eventually, the Lord will judge these matters to our satisfaction. Our unrighteous (selfish) anger must be extinguished. No room for resentment and rage will be found in a believer's heart if Christ is there!

Come unto Me, all ye that labor and are heavy laden, and I will give you rest. Take my yoke upon you, and learn of Me; for I am meek and lowly in heart: and ye shall find rest unto your souls. For My yoke is easy, and My burden is light (Mt. 11:28-30).

The Lord is *"meek and lowly in heart."* Adams Clarke comments with regard to Matthew 11:29: "Wherever pride and anger dwell, there is nothing but mental labor and agony; but, where the meekness and humility of Christ dwell, all is smooth, even, peaceable, and quiet; for the work of righteousness is peace, and the effect of righteousness, quietness and assurance forever."[1]

The picture on the front cover is of a lake in northwest Wisconsin which our home overlooks. For some reason beyond my comprehension but certainly not my appreciation, we are frequently blessed with spectacular sunrises and sunsets. The radiant hues and brilliant colors are simply majestic. This scene depicts the sun setting upon a peaceful heart and serene mind. May this picture represent your passion to end each day with all anger resolved. Seek grace from heaven, where not even a ripple intrudes upon the sea of glass encompassing the throne of majesty on high. The unfathomable and permanent counsels of Almighty God ensure nothing but peace there, and, nonetheless, His peace here, if we choose to lay hold of it.

Be angry, and do not sin: do not let the sun go down on your wrath (Eph. 4:26 NKVJ).

Endnotes

Preface

1. Warren Wiersbe, *The Bible Exposition Commentary, Vol. 2* (Victor Books, Wheaton, IL: 1989), Luke 15:25-28
2. Associated Press Wire Release (December 10, 2004).
3. Charles Spurgeon, *Spurgeon's Morning and Evening Devotions,* May 29 – Morning).
4. Raymond J. Larson, *Topical Encyclopedia of Living Quotations* (Bethany House Publishers, Minneapolis, MN: 1982)

Understanding Anger

1. Charles Dickens, *Oliver Twist* (Dood, Mead & Company; NY: 1941) pp. 55-56

God's Anger – Our Pattern

1. Warren Wiersbe, op. cit., Eccl. 12:14
2. H. A. Ironside, *Holiness – The False and the True* (Loizeaux, Neptune, NJ: 1912), p. 33
3. J. Oswald Sanders, *Spiritual Leadership* (Moody Press, Chicago, IL: 1980), p. 96
4. Warren Wiersbe, op. cit., James 1:19

Be Responsible

1. J. Oswald Sanders, op. cit., pp. 96-97

Anger Flavors

1. W. E. Vine, *Vine's Expository Dictionary of Biblical Words,* Thomas Nelson Publishers: 1985), Anger

Anger Flavors (cont.)
2. Edythe Draper, *Draper's Quotations from the Christian World –
   Soul* (Tyndale House Publishers Inc., Wheaton, Il. – electronic
   copy), Anger
3. Ibid., Anger
4. Dr. Les Carter and Dr. Frank Minirth, *The Anger Workbook*
   (Thomas Nelson Publishers, Nashville, TN: 1993), p. 27
5. Ibid., p. 31
6. Partly adapted from Dr. Richard P. Walters, *Anger Yours & Mine
   & What to Do About It* (Zondervan Publishing House, Grand
   Rapids, MI: 1981), p. 17

Investigating the Cause of Anger
1. Ibid., p. 35

Learning Christ
1. William MacDonald, *Believers' Bible Commentary* (Thomas
   Nelson Pub., Nashville, TN: 1995), p. 2304
2. Dr. Howard Taylor, *Spiritual Secret of Hudson Taylor*
   (Whitaker House, New Kensington, PA: 1996), p. 367

First-aid Techniques
1. Drapers Quotations, op. cit., Anger
2. Dr. Richard Walters, op. cit., p. 48
3. Dr. Howard Taylor, op. cit., p. 273
4. Charles Spurgeon, op. cit., April 22nd – Evening
5. Oswald Chambers, *My Utmost for His Highest*, (Discovery
   House, Grand Rapids, MI:1963), August 6

Deflate the Balloon
1. Warren Wiersbe, op. cit., 1 Timothy 4:8
2. Susan Boe, *Total Health Choices for a Winning Lifestyle,*
   (Riveredge Publishing Co., West Linn, Oregon: 1995), p.
   113
3. Drapers Quotations, op. cit., Laughter

Deflate the Balloon (cont.)
4. Ibid., Laughter
5. Ibid., Weeping
6. Ibid., Weeping

Seeking Forgiveness
1. Bob Laurent, Watchman Nee (Barbour Publishing, Inc. Uhrichsville, OH), p. 36
2. Warren Wiersbe, op. cit., Vol. 1, p. 238

The Cover
1. Adams Clarke, *Adams Clarke's Commentary* (Public Domain: biblestudyhelps.com) Mt. 11:29.